SNEAKY VEGGIES

How to Get Vegetables Under the Radar and into Your Family

CHRIS FISK

STERLING PUBLISHING CO., INC.

NEW YORK

To my mother, Trudy, who taught me how to cook and
how to laugh, and to my father, Stan, the Colonel, who
taught me covert operations with a side order of humor.

Library of Congress Cataloging-in-Publication Data

Fisk, Chris.
    Sneaky veggies : get vegetables under the radar and into your family / Chris Fisk.
        p. cm.
    Includes index.
    ISBN-13: 978-1-4027-2863-1
    ISBN-10: 1-4027-2863-8
    1. Cookery (Vegetables) I. Title.

TX801.F5282 2006
641.6'5--dc22

                                                     2005032098

2 4 6 8 10 9 7 5 3 1

Published by Sterling Publishing Co., Inc.
387 Park Avenue South, New York, NY 10016
© 2006 by Chris Fisk
Distributed in Canada by Sterling Publishing
c/o Canadian Manda Group, 165 Dufferin Street
Toronto, Ontario, Canada M6K 3H6
Distributed in the United Kingdom by GMC Distribution Services
Castle Place, 166 High Street, Lewes, East Sussex, England BN7 1XU
Distributed in Australia by Capricorn Link (Australia) Pty. Ltd.
P.O. Box 704, Windsor, NSW 2756, Australia

Sterling ISBN-13: 978-1-4027-2863-1
ISBN-10: 1-4027-2863-8

Book design by Richard Oriolo

For information about custom editions, special sales, premium and
corporate purchases, please contact Sterling Special Sales
Department at 800-805-5489 or specialsales@sterlingpub.com.

ACKNOWLEDGMENTS

First of all, I want to thank Chef Marina Valeriani, Chef Lynn Saathoff, and Chef Dan Silverman, my teachers. Your kindness and culinary acumen are the only reasons this book is possible. I must also thank all my students. You have taught me how to teach.

Craig Buckbee and Suzy Winkler, my neighbors, get a giant thank you for happily eating unnatural quantities of vegetables in various guises and giving honest feedback. Thanks to my sister Deedee Kornman, Melissa Welsh, Sue Suefert, Corrine Herlihy, Rick Pantaleoni, Ann Megyas, Julia Strohm, Christine Chiu, and John Hluchyj (you say it just the way it's spelled) for joyfully testing recipes for me. John has also consumed more of my food over the years than anyone, and with much zeal and appreciation—we all need a John around. Thanks to Abby Rabinowitz at Sterling for not only being immensely helpful, enthusiastic, and kind, but also for being the only person I know who *always* answers her phone. Special thanks to Tim Cockey and Beth Feldman for their skillful eyeballs–among their other parts.

Thanks to Bob Kornman, Dawn Dickstein, Amy Kara Schraub, Joanne Bennett, Dr. Wayne Yee, Mike Gillian, Ralph Dengler, Morten Clausen, Jonathan Taube, Marcus Fisk, Nelson and Sharyn Fisk, and Mark and Leslie Hazelwood for all your love and support over the years.

And finally, thanks to my nephews Patrick and Rawley Kornman, who will taste anything I ask them to.

CONTENTS

Side Dishes   56

Main Courses   79

Desserts

INTRODUCTION

Mission Nutrition

Which came first: The finicky eater or the parents who want their child to eat well? Your objective, trying to feed your family tasty and nutritious foods, can seem like mission impossible. We know how important it is to eat a balanced diet that includes plenty of vegetables but feel helpless against that most immovable of objects, a broccoli-hating child. Nobody wants to do battle with the ones we love. What to do? Subterfuge!

There are some who might bristle at the premise of this book, but I think all's fair in the care and feeding of children. To get a thimbleful of carrot into some kids is nothing short of a miracle. How can accomplishing that be bad? Kids don't like cauliflower, but that doesn't mean they won't eat it happily when it's been properly camouflaged and well seasoned. With a little expertise you can even get them to love it. In fact, you can get them to enjoy eating half the produce section by following the recipes here. Your mission, should you choose to accept it, is to feed your children well, whether they know it or not!

A UNITED FRONT

This is not strictly a "kids food" cookbook. When you have to cook three different meals to please all the palates at one sitting, all you have is a recipe for stress. Dinner in particular should be one meal shared by everyone. The recipes included here will appeal on many levels, and as long as you always include at least one familiar food with every meal, nobody will go hungry. A plate full of never-seen-before food would challenge anyone, so don't overdo the new.

Studies find that children who eat meals regularly with their family have higher grade point averages and are better adjusted. They also seem to suffer less from depression and drug problems. Who knew it could be so simple? Obviously mealtime needs to be a priority in your house. If too many activities are cutting into time together at the table, perhaps you should consider cutting back on a few activities.

SMALL VICTORIES

When you look at the ingredients list for some of the recipes, you might feel like you're getting only a tablespoon or two of vegetables into your children, but I say that's a whole tablespoon! Children are little people anyway, so a little goes a long way. Maybe your spouse isn't too keen on green either. You'll be just as happy to get a few more vegetables into him too. Every little bit helps.

RESTRICTED TACTICS

While I'm all in favor of being sneaky, I don't condone bribery or deal making—and neither do the experts. Children are naturally able to control the amount of food they need and will eat when they are hungry. If you force them to eat, they lose this natural ability and will not be driven by hunger—that's a bad thing. Making children eat broccoli in order to score chocolate cake could lead to eating disorders or food issues for the rest of their lives. So, three cheers for subterfuge!

SPECIAL MANEUVERS

When children are involved in the meal-making process they are more likely to eat that meal. You will have to balance between covering your tracks and allowing them to participate, but I find the average parent to be remarkably shrewd when necessary. There are lots of ways for kids to help. Reading a recipe aloud builds their confidence, and they'll learn some useful vocabulary words while being of help to you. Even a toddler can dump in the flour (you may have a bit more cleanup). Get them involved! I think the absolute best way to hook them is a trip to the farmer's market. It's an adventure and a fun family outing that helps support local farming. Let them choose one or two new things to try, and they will be vested in the meals using those ingredients.

I might be asking you to do a bit more cooking than you have been doing, especially if you have been relying on packaged foods, which really provide only the appearance of convenience and can be full of undesirable ingredients. I'm hoping that nourishing your children with the best food you can get into them will be inspiration enough. I always tell my students that cooking can be an extremely creative outlet. If you tire of having to do what the boss says all day long, try deviating from a recipe: "Chris says to use two cloves of garlic, but you know what? I'm going to use three. Ha!" I call this giving yourself a promotion.

INTELLIGENCE BREACH

If, perchance, you are found out in your culinary skullduggery and have some 'splainin' to do, you can employ the following damage control statements, depending on the nature of the discovery.

1   **I'm trying a new recipe.**

2   **That's a spice called foolenya, from the island of Hummina Hummina. Maybe we can go there someday. I hear they have a really big water slide there.**

3   **The pages of the cookbook were stuck together, and I didn't realize my mistake until the carrots went in!**

4   **Yeah, it does look kinda different. It's a new brand; I really like it. How 'bout you?**

THE BITE CLUB

Many families have "polite bite" policies. For some of the recipes that follow, success in your mission to get your family to eat and like vegetables depends on this policy, but it is also a way to reinforce good manners and, most important, respect for the cook. Membership in the Bite Club does not fall under the heading of bribery or battling at the table, just common courtesy. Keep in mind that children generally need to taste a new food five to ten times before liking it, and most parents give up after just a few tries. Enforcing the Bite Club rule will absolutely lead to successes eventually because continued exposure is crucial.

Children instinctively shy away from foreign and bitter foods. This dates back to the days when we foraged for dinner and ate in a cave, when eating the wrong thing could be fatal. Explains a lot, eh? My life was forever changed when I was nine and my grandmother made me eat a bite of green pepper, which I knew I didn't like. Boy, was I wrong, and a new favorite food was discovered.

THE ARSENAL

To properly execute the recipes in this book you will need to have a few essential items, including a poker face.

You will need a blender and a food processor. Food processors are generally used for solid foods, and blenders are generally used for liquids. I'm fond of the machines that are a combo of the two. I rely heavily on my mini food processor, and you'll find it an adequate fit for holding the ingredients of many of the recipes. Some food processors come with two or three sizes of work bowls that are handy as well. You can generally make do with just a blender, but you'll have to pulse and scrape a bit more.

Some of the recipes suggest using a mandoline. This is a great little gadget that makes especially thin, perfect slices of potatoes, carrots, and other veggies. There are many models to choose from. I prefer the plastic or "Japanese" mandoline. Be extra careful when using it, though, because you will be waving your fingers over an extremely sharp blade. A mandoline costs between $20 and $250.

Only one of the recipes calls for a spiral slicer, but you can't believe how much fun it is to use. Kids over the age of seven should be able to help you spiral slice, and since this is simply about a fun shape rather than sneakiness, you can get them involved. Things like radishes, zucchini, turnips, and butternut squash are truly transformed by a spiral slicer. Once you start spiraling, you can't stop! These retail for $20 to $45.

PROCUREMENT

To get in and out of the grocery quickly, a good shopping list is essential. Start your list with the following headings: Produce, Meat, Dairy, and Grocery. Organize your list to match the setup of your grocery store. This will speed up the whole process and keep you from having to return to aisle three at the end. At my market, they keep the rotisserie chickens in a funny place, so I find I have to write "Rotisserie Chicken" in the middle of the page in order to remember it, because it doesn't fall under any of the headings. You might have a similar idiosyncrasy in your market to contend with.

THE MAJOR OPERATIVES

You will find that a large number of recipes call for cauliflower, carrots, and parsnips. There are a few reasons for this. First, they are easily found in most markets and camouflage well. Because of their white color, cauliflower and parsnips disappear quite readily, and carrots match a number of food backdrops nicely. Second, carrots and parsnips are slightly sweet—need I say more when it comes to what children like? All three veggies possess excellent nutritional profiles. Parsnips are a good source of vitamin C and folate and also contain soluble fiber, which seems to lower bad cholesterol. Cauliflower is an impressive source of vitamin C, a good source of folate and vitamin B_6, and is cruciferous, meaning it contains a number of phytochemicals that promote good health. Carrots are an exceptional source of carotenoids and contain vitamin B_6 and fiber.

UNUSUAL SUSPECTS

Most of the recipes feature your garden-variety veggies. In some of the recipes, though, I have employed a few less glamorous or noteworthy vegetables. It might even be the first you've heard of or tasted some of them. The idea is that it will be helpful to have sneaky vegetables lying around—ones that aren't particularly recognizable. Make friends with the produce man and woman; they will be great allies on your mission. They can order things for you, or perhaps simply identify previously unknown vegetables. They also frequently have tips for handling, storage, and even recipes. Most important, if you ask sweetly, they will almost always "look in the back" for you when you can't find something.

When you come across kohlrabi, Jerusalem artichokes, or jicama in a recipe, don't run off to the safety of a carrot recipe out of fear! These are almost certainly lurking in your produce section just waiting to be discovered. I have explained in each recipe all you'll need to know about cooking with them. To prepare jicama (pronounced "HICK-ah-ma"), you simply peel and eat, and it's an amazing source of vitamin C. Jerusalem artichokes or "sunchokes" are chock-full of B vitamins, iron, and fiber. Kohlrabi ("coal-ROB-ee") is cruciferous, and as you read the recipes, it will become clear that I want everyone to eat more cruciferous vegetables.

FIELD OPERATIONS

Organic may have advantages over conventionally grown produce, but if it cuts into other important expenses, just remember that the most important thing is eating a variety of fruits and vegetables. In general, I let my budget dictate which way I go.

Always wash vegetables before preparing. This is for general cleanliness, as you don't know where your produce has been. I have been known to wash peppers with a whisper of dish soap, because their skins are oiled to keep them fresh longer. Never use dish soap if the skin is broken, however, and rinse them well to remove any traces of the soap. Fresh leafy greens should be put in a large bowl of tepid water and left to soak briefly. Pull the greens out of the water, leaving any dirt or sand behind. Arugula, cilantro, spinach, and other especially dirty or sandy greens should be washed in a few changes of water. There's nothing worse than a gritty green!

HANDLING OF OPERATIVES

Many of the recipes will ask that the vegetables be cooked until tender. It is important that the vegetables be tender for them to properly disappear into the dish. Cut them all into approximately the same size pieces to ensure even cooking (a larger piece of carrot will take longer to cook than a smaller piece). To test for tenderness, poke veggies with a paring knife.

The recipes employing the blender or food processor will ask you to "puree until smooth," and this too is important. He who rushes leaves telltale chunks, and then the jig is up.

MUNITIONS CACHE

To streamline cooking on school nights you might think about making a puree stash of the more frequently used vegetables like parsnips, carrots, and cauliflower. Most purees will keep for three days in the fridge or can be frozen for up to two months. Having these made ahead will not only bring the recipes together more quickly, it will also make cleanup easier because you can steam all the vegetables using one pot and simply give the food processor or blender a quick rinse between vegetables.

If you find your energy and freezer inventory flagging during some particularly busy time of year, and your budget allows for it, you can pick up a few jars of baby food vegetables. Use them as a shortcut in some of the recipes here, or sneak them into your family usuals.

SOUP STRATEGY

I rely heavily on soup for my subterfuge for several reasons. For starters, soup is the easiest place to hide vegetables. It is also a nutritional font because all the goodness stays in the pot. In some countries soup is served every day. Wouldn't it be a great custom to adopt in your house? Starting dinner with a lovely bowl of goodness is a boon because your family will be hungry and more likely to eat it, and you can worry less about what they eat during the rest of the meal. Assign a night of the week for your children to pick which soup to serve—get them involved!

FLAVOR INFILTRATION

The art of seasoning seems a bit mysterious to many cooks. I'm going to clear it up right here, right now. You start with salt. If you aren't sure, it almost always needs a little more salt. Time and again my students have expressed great surprise at how transforming salt can be. I don't call for salt in my ingredients list because I assume you have it on hand. I want you to put in as little or as much as *you* feel the dish needs. I like kosher salt because it is coarse, which makes it easy to see how much you are using. If, after you have added salt, the dish just seems to taste a bit saltier, then you "go for an acid." By this I mean that you should add something like fresh lemon juice, vinegar, or wine. The acid brightens up the flavors and gives a bit of wow. If after you have added salt and acid it still doesn't have soul, try something sweet: honey, sugar, or jelly. Ketchup is a sweet acid and Dijon mustard is a salty acid. Each is good for killing two birds with one stone and can do wonders for a pot of soup. The most important thing is to taste before serving and to trust yourself to know what tastes good! When the waiter places your food in front of you, do you ask him to tell you if it tastes good? Trust yourself.

As long as you don't have high blood pressure or are predisposed to it, adding salt during the cooking process doesn't contribute significantly to overall sodium intake. Processed foods, on the other hand, are full of sodium. This is especially true of snack foods and "dinner in the box" items, so read those labels.

You know that everything tastes better with a little butter, but I'll bet you didn't know there was chemistry involved. The bitterness in greens breaks down when combined with fat, and our friend salt helps to block the bitterness. Don't skip certain recipes simply because they rely on butter or cheese, and don't arbitrarily skimp on the salt. We are trying to get children to taste, eat, and eventually *like* vegetables. There is a direct correlation between expectation and perception. If they see cheese, they might expect to like what's under it, and what you're thinking greatly effects how things taste. Remember that time you were thinking about coffee and took a sip of lemonade? Shocking! The food companies and others in the business of feeding know this too. Have you noticed that prunes have become dried plums in the market? Chilean sea bass always used to be known as Patagonian Toothfish—yum! That's what I call a marketing makeover. We, on the other hand, are going to give a truly meaningful makeover to vegetables.

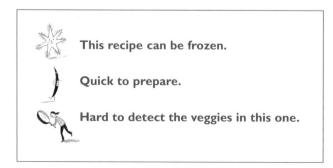

This recipe can be frozen.

Quick to prepare.

Hard to detect the veggies in this one.

SNACKS, SAUCES, AND DRESSINGS

HIDDEN VEGGIE RANCH DRESSING

What would we do without ranch dressing? To cheat, simply puree steamed parsnips with regular ranch dressing in the blender. Maybe start with just one parsnip at first. Tell them it's a new brand. The family of a friend of mine loves this warm over chicken or fish.

MAKES ABOUT 2 CUPS

2 medium parsnips, peeled and sliced thinly

$^3/_4$–1 cup buttermilk, depending on thickness desired

4 tablespoons reduced-fat mayonnaise

$^1/_2$ teaspoon garlic powder or $^1/_2$ clove fresh

1 teaspoon dried or fresh dill

12 leaves fresh basil or 1 teaspoon dried

1 tablespoon vinegar (rice, red wine, or apple cider)

1 chopped scallion, optional

Steam the parsnips in a saucepan with a little water until tender, about 10 minutes.

Place parsnips in the blender with the buttermilk, mayonnaise, and garlic, then puree until smooth. Season with salt and add remaining ingredients. Add scallion, if using, and pulse a few times. (If you puree it completely the dressing will turn green, and real ranch dressing ain't green!) Taste and adjust seasoning. Refrigerate for at least 1 hour.

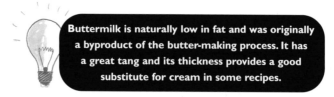

Buttermilk is naturally low in fat and was originally a byproduct of the butter-making process. It has a great tang and its thickness provides a good substitute for cream in some recipes.

ROASTED RED PEPPER SAUCE/DRESSING

It's just this easy to make a vegetable disappear. Use this on grilled chicken or fish, as dressing, or in sandwiches.

MAKES ABOUT I CUP

$^1/_2$ cup favorite vinaigrette or dressing (Italian, ranch)

I roasted red pepper, about 4 ounces (sometimes called pimiento)

$^1/_2$ teaspoon sugar or honey

Place everything in the blender and puree until smooth. Taste and season with salt if needed. Keeps 2 weeks in the refrigerator.

> Peppers are a good source of vitamins A and C. You can use strips of roasted peppers or pimientos in place of mayonnaise in sandwiches. Peppers add moisture that the mayo would have supplied.

CREAMY SANDWICH
SPREAD

Talk about killing two birds with one stone: We're removing some fat and adding a virtuous vegetable! Use this anywhere mayonnaise is called for or anytime you would ordinarily reach for mayo. If you fear your family is too accustomed to the real thing, you can bump up the mayo at first and then start using less every time you make this. It isn't quite as smooth as mayonnaise, but it is really yummy. Because it freezes well and is also called for in several recipes that follow, make a double batch.

MAKES ABOUT 1 1/2 CUPS

One 10-ounce box frozen cauliflower, defrosted
1/4 cup buttermilk
3–5 tablespoons mayonnaise
2 teaspoons rice vinegar

Squeeze the cauliflower to remove excess water, and place in the food processor. Add the buttermilk, mayonnaise, rice vinegar, and salt. Puree until smooth, then taste, adding more mayonnaise if needed. Keeps 2 weeks in the fridge or freezer. Stir back together after defrosting if needed.

NOTE To make the spread a little smoother you can steam the cauliflower for about 5 minutes first. Let it cool, and then continue as above.

"They" have finally decided that frozen vegetables are probably nutritionally superior to fresh. This is because vegetables are frozen soon after harvest, which locks in the nutrients. Produce from a local farmer's market is also desirable because it hasn't traveled great distances, and therefore hasn't lost nutritional value along the way.

ROCKIN' TARTAR SAUCE

This has a great tang that everyone will love, but it is much lower in fat than traditional tartar sauce—yeah! All my tasters like it better.

MAKES ABOUT $^1/_2$ CUP

$^1/_4$ cup I Call It Dreamy: Creamy Sandwich Spread (page 18)

2–3 tablespoons buttermilk

Juice of $^1/_2$ lemon or 2 teaspoons rice vinegar

2 teaspoons pickle relish, optional

In a small bowl, stir everything together. Taste, adding more buttermilk to thin if desired, and serve with your favorite fish main course.

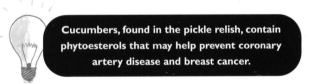

Cucumbers, found in the pickle relish, contain phytoesterols that may help prevent coronary artery disease and breast cancer.

BASIL DIP

This is green, but dipping is just so much fun that I find one taste is all it takes. It's also great at parties served with fancier crudités.

1 cup I Call It Dreamy: Creamy Sandwich Spread (page 18)
1 bunch basil, washed and stems removed
1 teaspoon rice vinegar

In a food processor place the creamy sandwich spread and as many basil leaves as will fit. Pulse several times and add remaining basil leaves and vinegar. Puree until smooth. Taste and season with salt if needed. Serve with baby carrots, pitas, or other favorite dipping items. Keeps 1 week in the refrigerator.

Throw way that bottle of lemon juice in your fridge. It doesn't even resemble lemon juice, which oxidizes very quickly. If you don't believe me, have a taste! Instead, use about half the amount called for of rice vinegar, a mild acid that will give the same kick as the lemon would. Now, if you're making a lemon meringue pie, you're going to have to go out and buy lemons.

ROASTED GARLIC AND RED PEPPER HUMMUS

Full of vitamin A, folic acid, and our friend fiber, this dip looks like it might actually be full of cheese because of the roasted red peppers. Roasting the garlic is a little bit of work, but it gives the dip an amazing flavor that everyone will love. Substitute a clove of chopped raw garlic if you are pressed for time. Serve with pita points, baby carrots, or, if desperate, tortilla chips.

MAKES 8 SERVINGS

1 head garlic

3 tablespoons olive oil, divided

One 15-ounce can garbanzo beans, drained

One 6-ounce jar roasted red peppers or pimientos, drained

1–2 tablespoons rice vinegar

1 tablespoon cumin

Preheat the oven to 325°F.

Cut about ½ inch off the top of the garlic. Place on a 12-inch square of foil and drizzle with 1 tablespoon of the oil. Wrap garlic in the foil and bake for 1 hour or until the cloves are tender (check with a paring knife). Let cool and squeeze cloves out of their skins.

Put 3–6 cloves of the roasted garlic and the remaining ingredients in the food processor and puree until smooth, about 2 minutes. Season with salt and puree another 20 seconds. It will taste even better in a day or two. Will keep up to 2 weeks refrigerated. Leaving children alone with the dip and the threat that "it's only for the big people" is sometimes fun.

NOTE Leftover garlic can be kept refrigerated for 1 week in a baggie. Use it in mashed potatoes, salad dressings, sauces, and with pasta.

PARMESAN BROCCOLI DIP

Broccoli has the **PR** problem of being green, but if you can get them to taste this, you're in. This is absolutely the tastiest way to eat broccoli, perhaps the most virtuous veggie. I might even consider using **Chee·tos** to get them to try it because broccoli is one awesome vegetable. Start with baby carrots, sliced zucchini, or pita bread, though.

MAKES ABOUT 4 SERVINGS

$1/2$ head broccoli, stems trimmed

$1/2$ medium onion, chopped

I clove garlic, chopped, or more if it's cold and flu season

$1/4$ cup **Parmesan cheese**, or more if necessary

Steam broccoli in a medium saucepan with a little water until tender, about 8 minutes.

Heat a skillet over medium heat. Add just enough oil to coat the bottom of the pan. Add the onions and garlic, and cook until onions are softened, about 3 minutes. Don't let the garlic burn.

Put broccoli, onion, and garlic in the food processor and process until the broccoli is coarsely chopped and no large pieces of stem remain, about 30 seconds. Add the Parmesan and continue to process until smooth. Season with salt and taste! It tastes best warm. It also makes a great filling for a sandwich the next day.

> Parmesan is a good source of calcium and is low in fat, so let them sprinkle it liberally on anything you're trying to get them to eat.

PURPLE CAULIFLOWER DIP

This is way better than paste, so ask your produce man/woman to order purple cauliflower for you.

MAKES 4 SERVINGS

¹/₄ head purple cauliflower, cut into florets
1 tablespoon reduced-fat mayonnaise
3 tablespoons reduced-fat cream cheese
1 teaspoon rice vinegar

Steam cauliflower in a saucepan with a little water until tender, about 8 minutes. Place in the food processor and add remaining ingredients, then process until smooth. Season with salt and taste, adjusting as needed. Serve with anything—it's cauliflower! Will keep 1 week in the refrigerator.

The purple color comes from anthocyanins, the same component found in the skin of grapes and in red cabbage, which appear to protect the heart.

ARTICHOKE TOASTS

Nutritionally speaking, artichokes are unsung little vegetables, and tasty too! I like marinated artichokes because somebody else very kindly added all the flavoring needed.

MAKES 2 SERVINGS

2 pieces bread (whole grain if possible)
One 4-ounce jar marinated artichoke hearts, drained
2 tablespoons Parmesan cheese

Preheat the broiler or toaster oven.

For crunchier toasts, toast the bread briefly before topping.

Coarsely chop the artichokes or, for especially picky eaters and to make it easier to eat, place the artichokes into a mini food processor and pulse several times. Distribute artichokes between the two pieces of bread and smooth out. Dust with Parmesan cheese and place in toaster oven or under the broiler for about 1 minute or until just golden brown. Cut into charming triangles just like my mom used to do.

If needed, you may use a more dramatic cheese like Cheddar and use a little less artichoke until the kids realize they like the toasts.

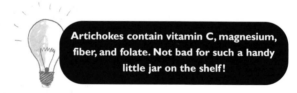

Artichokes contain vitamin C, magnesium, fiber, and folate. Not bad for such a handy little jar on the shelf!

ASPARAGUS WITH FAVORITE DIP

Not so sneaky really, but if you can get to the kids when they are young enough, you'll have them loving asparagus. A whole spear can be well played with before being eaten, and my belief is that the favorite dip is tempting enough. The whisper of butter helps get them over the hurdle in the beginning. Start leaving the butter out once they're hooked.

MAKES 2 SERVINGS

1/2 bunch asparagus, ends trimmed

1 teaspoon butter

1/4 cup favorite dip (see Hidden Veggie Ranch Dressing, page 16)

Heat a small skillet with just enough water to cover the asparagus. When water is boiling, add a little salt, the asparagus, and the butter. Let cook for 2–3 minutes, and then remove from the skillet and serve alongside dip. Save any leftover asparagus for the soup pot.

One serving of asparagus contains a large percentage of your daily recommended folate, which helps cell growth and repair. It is also a good source of vitamin C and rich in antioxidants that promote health.

ARTICHOKE DIP

It takes only 2 minutes to make this dip and an hour to bake cookies.... You choose. Serve with a nutritious dippable: whole grain crackers, pita points, or baby carrots.

MAKES 4 SERVINGS

Two 4-ounce jars marinated artichoke hearts, mostly drained
1 tablespoon reduced-fat mayonnaise
1 tablespoon reduced-fat sour cream or yogurt

In the bowl of a mini food processor, combine all the ingredients. Puree until smooth. Taste and season with salt.

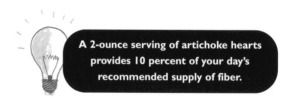

A 2-ounce serving of artichoke hearts provides 10 percent of your day's recommended supply of fiber.

CHEESY CAULIFLOWER NACHOS

Let's face it, nachos are a fact of life. The fact is that kids will like them even better with a little something extra. You can serve this the next time you host a sleepover and then brag to Billy's mother about how her son just loves your cauliflower.

Half a 10-ounce box frozen cauliflower, defrosted

$^1/_2$ cup chicken or vegetable broth

4 ounces Cheddar cheese, grated

Corn chips (look for the baked ones)

In a perfect world you would be able to add:

$^1/_4$ cup drained black beans

$^1/_4$ cup guacamole

$^1/_2$ cup salsa

Chopped scallions or cilantro

Heat a small saucepan over medium-high heat with the cauliflower and the chicken broth. Bring to a boil, then reduce heat and let simmer 5 minutes, or until tender. Transfer to the blender and puree until smooth. Add the cheese and puree again. Return to the saucepan to reheat if needed.

Arrange corn chips on a plate. Drizzle cheese sauce over chips and add as many other nutritious toppings as you are able.

While avocados are known for their fat content, it is primarily the heart-healthy monounsaturated variety. Avocados are also a good source of fiber, and they contain the phytochemical lutein, which promotes eye health and may slow down thickening of arteries. Go guac!

NO-NAME BEEF ROLL-UPS

These could be served as a main course for dinner on a night when it's too hot to cook. They'd also be good in a lunch box. If the kiddos will derive pleasure from removing the arugula, use it; otherwise, just put it on for the big people.

12 ounces good deli roast beef (hopefully not sliced by the new guy)
¹/₂ cup I Call It Dreamy: Creamy Sandwich Spread (page 18)
1–2 tablespoons horseradish sauce, optional
¹/₂ bunch arugula, large stems removed, optional

Lay out the slices of roast beef. Spread on a small amount of I Call It Dreamy: Creamy Sandwich Spread. If using, top that with a little horseradish sauce. Lay a few leaves of arugula on top and roll. These may be assembled a few hours ahead and refrigerated. If you have fancy toothpicks, you can use them to secure the roll-ups and to add a little drama to the presentation.

ALL-PURPOSE (PERFECTLY SMOOTH) TOMATO CARROT SAUCE

Beyond saving you money and containing wholesome ingredients, this tomato sauce tastes better than anything in a jar at the store.

MAKES ABOUT 3 CUPS

I medium onion, chopped

2 cloves garlic, chopped

One 15-ounce can crushed tomatoes

2 carrots, thinly sliced

I teaspoon sugar

I teaspoon basil

$^{1}/_{2}$ teaspoon thyme

I teaspoon oregano or marjoram

Heat a skillet over medium-high heat. Add just enough oil to coat the bottom of the pan, then add the onion. Cook until onions are just turning golden. Add garlic and cook another minute. Don't let the garlic burn. Add the tomatoes, carrots, sugar, and herbs, then season with salt and stir. Let cook about 15 minutes or until the carrots are tender. Remove from heat and let cool slightly. Transfer sauce to the blender and puree until smooth. Taste and adjust seasoning. It keeps for 2 weeks in the refrigerator, and it freezes well.

Beta-carotene isn't heat sensitive, so all the goodness stays put when cooked. Yeah!

CRAFTILY CRUCIFEROUS CHEESE SAUCE

I am the daughter of a man who will only eat broccoli when it's drowned in cheese. Is it any wonder I wrote this book? Start adding an extra floret after a while. Although the real purpose of this sauce is to make any vegetable more attractive, feel free to douse chicken, bread, or anything you'd like with it.

MAKES ABOUT I CUP

4 cauliflower florets
$\frac{1}{2}$ cup chicken or vegetable broth
4 ounces Cheddar cheese, grated

Heat a small saucepan over medium-high heat with the cauliflower and the broth. Bring to a boil, then reduce heat and let simmer about 8 minutes or until tender. Transfer to the blender and puree until smooth. Add the cheese and puree again. Keeps 1 week in the refrigerator and can be frozen.

I tell students that the word *cruciferous* comes from Latin meaning "to live forever when consumed," but then I confess that it actually refers to plants in the mustard family and how they grow. You will, however, truly enjoy many benefits from eating more cruciferous veggies.

PARSNIP STACKS

This is a riff on an elegant first-course Napoleon I've served for years. They can be eaten with a fork, but I think fingers are the way to go. The kids will love stacking these themselves. Try making it with one carrot and one parsnip, and then alternate the colors of the layers. Dare I hope for zucchini slices someday?

MAKES 2 SERVINGS

2 parsnips, peeled

2 teaspoons canola or grape seed oil

3–4 tablespoons Hidden Veggie Ranch Dressing (page 16)

Preheat the oven to 425°F. Line a cookie sheet or jelly roll pan with parchment or foil (shiny side down).

Using a mandoline or carefully with a knife, slice the parsnips into even $\frac{1}{8}$-inch slices. Place slices in a bowl and toss with the oil. Lay the slices out on the cookie sheet, season with salt, and place in the oven for 15 minutes or until golden and tender. Remove from the oven and let cool.

To assemble the stacks, take the four largest slices and top with a tiny dollop of dressing, followed by a slightly smaller slice. Repeat until all the slices are layered on.

Skip the stacking! Just serve parsnip chips on the side or as a snack.

SWEET POTATO CORN BREAD

This makes a nice afternoon snack on a chilly day, or you can serve it with a soupy, stewy main course, of course. To cheat, simply add the grated sweet potato to your favorite brand of corn bread mix.

MAKES 8–10 SERVINGS

1 cup all-purpose flour

1 cup cornmeal

1/4 cup sugar

1 tablespoon baking powder

1 teaspoon salt

1/4 cup (1/2 stick) butter

1 egg, lightly beaten

1 cup buttermilk

1 sweet potato, peeled and grated

Preheat oven to 425°F. Butter, oil, or spray a 9 × 9 inch baking dish.

In a large bowl, combine flour, cornmeal, sugar, baking powder, and salt. Using two forks or a pastry cutter, cut the butter into the mixture until crumbly. In a small bowl, stir together the egg, buttermilk, and sweet potato, then pour into flour mixture. Stir until just blended. Pour into prepared baking dish. Bake 20 minutes or until the center springs back when lightly pressed with a fingertip. Cool in the pan on a wire rack.

Confused about yams and sweet potatoes? Join the club. They are both in the sweet potato family and can generally be used interchangeably. The confusion arose when the darker-fleshed variety was introduced several decades ago. The producers wanted to differentiate it from the light-fleshed varieties and decided on the name yam. Yam was derived from the African word *Nyami*, referring to the edible root also known as taro. An African yam is quite a different beast altogether, but since taro is seldom seen in traditional markets, you needn't worry.

FONDUE WITH VEGETABLES FOR DIPPING

Fondue means "melt" in French, and we all do when it comes to cheese. This is a classic way to get kids to try new vegetables. Be sure to put two florets of broccoli out to dunk when they run out of the other stuff.

1 clove garlic, cut in half
$^1/_2$ cup white wine*
Juice of $^1/_2$ lemon
8 ounces Gruyère or imported Swiss cheese, grated
2 teaspoons cornstarch
Baby carrots, apple and pear wedges, broccoli or cauliflower florets

Rub the inside of a small saucepan with the garlic and leave in the pan. Add the wine and lemon juice, season with salt, and place over medium heat.

Toss the cheese with the cornstarch in a bowl. Just as the wine reaches a boil, slowly add the cheese to the pot, stirring constantly until the cheese is melted and smooth. Continue stirring another minute or until thickened slightly, then let them have at it! If the cheese begins to firm up too much, just whisk over medium heat briefly.

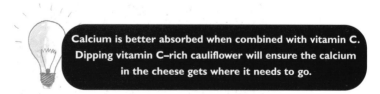

Calcium is better absorbed when combined with vitamin C. Dipping vitamin C–rich cauliflower will ensure the calcium in the cheese gets where it needs to go.

* You may substitute chicken or vegetable broth for the wine if desired.

SWEET POTATO FRIES

I'm calling these a snack, but they would certainly make a great side dish. They don't get crunchy like regular fries, but they're tasty and fun to eat.

MAKES 4 SERVINGS

2 sweet potatoes, peeled and cut into 2-inch-long fries
1 tablespoon canola or grape seed oil

Preheat oven to 450°F.

For easy cleanup line the cookie sheet or jelly roll pan with parchment or foil (shiny side down). Toss, spray, or brush fries with oil and lay out on the sheet pan, trying not to crowd them. Season fries with salt. Fries can be held at this point for up to 2 hours.

Place in the oven for 12–15 minutes or until golden brown and tender. EAT! Puree any leftovers into a soup, sauce, or hummus.

Sweet potatoes are high in vitamin A and a good source of vitamin B_6, potassium, and fiber.

CAULIFLOWER QUESADILLAS

Initially you might have to use less cauliflower, but the cheese does disguise it nicely. The small holes on a standard grater will make really nice tiny bits of cauliflower.

MAKES 4 SERVINGS

8 small flour tortillas
2 ounces Monterey Jack cheese, grated
$^1/_4$ head cauliflower, grated
$^1/_4$ cup salsa, I hope

Lay out 4 tortillas and top with half the cheese. Sprinkle on the cauliflower and top with the rest of the cheese and the remaining tortillas. Place on a griddle or in a skillet over medium heat until cheese is just melted. Remove and let cool slightly before cutting into wedges. Top with salsa if possible for another dose of veggies.

To get another little something into them, use corn tortillas rather than flour. Just lightly toast them over the burner (gas or electric) using tongs and then follow the recipe. They won't be as hard to eat as those prefab taco shells.

SOUPS

VEGETABLE BROTH

Soup is rich in a variety of vitamins and other goodies. If you can get nothing else past your family, you'll get this one into them. Make sure you have it on hand at all times, and know that homemade is far superior to store bought, both nutritionally and in flavor. Anytime a recipe calls for chicken broth, you can use this instead. They'll be getting at least a little something from the vegetable kingdom.

I keep a zipper bag in the freezer, and every time I have a tomato top, an onion bottom, or the stems of asparagus or broccoli, anything really, I pop it into the bag. Don't overdo things like cabbage or broccoli as they have a more pronounced flavor. When I have enough vegetable "trash" I make broth. If you are cooking with any regularity, you should be able to make this once a month easily. You can also add things straight from the fridge that are a bit past their prime or, if really desperate, buy a selection of fresh vegetables to make broth.

MAKES 2 TO 4 QUARTS

About 8 quarts vegetable pieces (2 large freezer bags full)
Water to cover by about 2 inches

Place vegetables in a large soup pot or two smaller pots and cover with water. Place over medium-high heat and bring to a boil. Reduce heat and let simmer for about 45 minutes. Strain out vegetables and let broth cool before placing in small containers and freezing.

ALPHABET SOUP

Soup can camouflage a variety of nutritious ingredients—in this case vitamin **A** and beta-carotene. The deep orange combines beautifully with tomato, rendering it imperceptible. The garlic and onion are pureed to create a smooth soup very much like what comes out of the can. Use leftover pumpkin for a **Who Wants a Milkshake? Pumpkin Smoothie** (page 122) or in **Quit Your Loafin' and Eat This Pumpkin Walnut Loaf** (page 117).

MAKES 4 SERVINGS

$^1/_2$ medium onion, chopped

1 clove garlic, chopped

One 14$^1/_2$-ounce can chicken broth, divided

2 tablespoons tomato paste

$^1/_4$ cup canned pumpkin (not pumpkin pie mix)

2 teaspoons sugar

2 tablespoons alphabet pasta

Heat a medium saucepan over medium heat. Add just enough oil to coat the bottom, then add the onion and cook until softened, about 3 minutes. Add the garlic and cook another 30 seconds, making sure the garlic doesn't burn. Remove from the heat and place onion and garlic in the blender with about $\frac{1}{4}$ cup chicken broth, then puree until smooth.

Place remaining chicken broth in a saucepan over medium heat. Add onion mixture, tomato paste, and pumpkin. Whisk until smooth and bring to a simmer. Add sugar and season with salt. Add pasta and let simmer 10 minutes, or until cooked. Taste, adding more sugar or salt if needed.

To serve, ladle soup into bowls and never let them see you sweat.

Sometimes there just isn't time for homemade soup. You can whisk one or two tablespoons of pumpkin into any tomato-based canned soup. Try vegetable soup if the members of your family aren't overly suspicious types.

TOMATO SOUP WITH CHEESE AND CARROT

A big cheat, but we don't want "too tired to cook" to translate into a vegetable-less meal.

MAKES 2 SERVINGS

I can favorite tomato soup
I carrot, peeled and thinly sliced
I ounce Cheddar cheese, grated

Heat a small saucepan over medium heat. Prepare the soup according to the directions on the label, adding the carrots to the pot. Let simmer about 10 minutes or until carrots are tender. Let cool slightly (hot soup will try to escape the blender, potentially causing a mess or injury), then transfer to the blender and puree until smooth. Return soup to the pot to reheat. Ladle into bowls and top with cheese. Sleep soundly.

> Tomatoes are rich in lycopene, an antioxidant that is credited with cancer prevention. Cooking tomatoes concentrates the lycopene.

BROCCOLI CHEDDAR SOUP

We have to try, don't we? Broccoli is just so full of the good stuff that the cheese is worth it.

MAKES 4 SERVINGS

2 tablespoons butter

1 onion, finely chopped

2 tablespoons all-purpose flour

2 cups chicken broth

One 10-ounce box frozen chopped broccoli, defrosted

8 ounces mild Cheddar cheese, grated

1 1/2 cups buttermilk

Heat a large saucepan over medium heat. Add the butter, then add the onions and let cook until softened, about 3 minutes. Add the flour and stir until smooth. Stir in the broth and continue stirring until well combined. Add the broccoli and bring to a boil, reduce to a simmer, and let cook 6–8 minutes or until the broccoli is tender.

Stir in the cheese and continue stirring until smooth and melted. Stir in buttermilk and let cook 1 minute, then taste and season with salt if desired. Remove from heat, ladle into bowls, and cross your fingers.

PURPLE CAULIFLOWER SOUP

Unlike so many purple vegetables, purple cauliflower holds its color when cooked! This recipe is a real treat in my book and always in my freezer.

MAKES 6 SERVINGS

1 medium onion, chopped

3 cloves garlic, chopped

4 cups chicken or vegetable broth

1 head purple cauliflower, cut into florets

1/4 cup buttermilk or yogurt

Heat a soup pot over medium-high heat. Add just enough oil to coat the bottom of the pan, then add the onion and cook until softened. Add garlic and cook another minute, making sure the garlic doesn't burn.

Add the broth and cauliflower and season with salt. Bring to a boil, then reduce the heat and let simmer for 8 minutes or until cauliflower is tender. Remove from the heat and let cool slightly (hot soup will try to escape the blender, potentially causing a mess or injury). Place soup in blender and puree until smooth. Return mixture to the pot over medium heat, then taste and adjust seasoning. Ladle into bowls and garnish with buttermilk or yogurt.

To make a pretty heart design with the buttermilk or yogurt, make a ring of tiny drips or dollops around the edge of the soup bowl. Take a skewer or toothpick and trace a circle through each drip or dollop. Voilà!

BEAN WITH BACON SOUP

Bean with bacon was my all-time favorite childhood soup. This show-stopper isn't just sneaky, it's yummy and good enough for guests.

MAKES 4–6 SERVINGS

3 strips bacon (turkey or regular), chopped

1 medium onion, chopped

2 cloves garlic, chopped

1 large sweet potato, peeled and cut into 1-inch pieces

2–3 cups chicken broth, divided

1 can small white beans, drained

2 tablespoons honey

Heat a large saucepan over medium-high heat. Add the bacon and cook, stirring often, until well browned and crispy. Remove to a paper towel and drain excess fat from the pan.

Return the pan to the heat and add the onion. Cook until just starting to turn golden, then add the garlic and cook another minute, making sure the garlic doesn't burn. Add the sweet potato and 2 cups of the chicken broth, then stir. Bring to a boil, then reduce to a simmer and let cook about 10–12 minutes or until potatoes are tender.

Remove from heat and let cool slightly (hot soup will try to escape the blender, potentially causing a mess or injury). Transfer to the blender and add half or all of the beans, depending on your family's preference. Puree until smooth and return to the pot. Add honey and season with salt, then taste and adjust seasoning as needed. Add any remaining beans and the cooked bacon, then stir to combine. Add remaining chicken broth if desired to thin the soup. Enjoy!

Beans make for great jokes in my classes, but heart disease, diabetes, cancer, diverticulitis, and birth defects can all be avoided by eating more of these nutrition all-stars. The "effects" of the beans diminish as your system adjusts to their regular consumption.

CREAMY CHICKEN AND RICE SOUP

Fat out, vegetables in! There's nothing better than a guilt-free creamy soup, and because the chicken is cooked on the bone, this soup is especially tasty. If onions are a problem, you can simmer them with the parsnips and puree them at the same time.

MAKES 8 SERVINGS

2 parsnips, peeled and thinly sliced

4 cups chicken broth, divided

1 medium onion, finely chopped

2 medium carrots, sliced

2 stalks celery, finely chopped

1 chicken, cut up and skinned, or 6 skinless thighs

1 teaspoon poultry seasoning

$1/2$ cup rice

2 tablespoons yogurt or reduced-fat sour cream, optional

In a soup pot or large saucepan, place the parsnips and 1 cup chicken broth. Bring to a boil, then reduce to a simmer. Let cook about 10 minutes or until parsnips are tender. Let cool slightly (hot soup will try to escape the blender, potentially causing a mess or injury). Transfer to a blender and puree until smooth.

In the same pot, use just enough oil to coat the bottom of the pan and add the onion. Let the onions cook until softened, about 3 minutes, then add the carrots and celery and cook another 2 minutes. Add the chicken, 4 cups of water, remaining chicken broth, and poultry seasoning to the pot, and season with salt. Bring to a boil, then reduce the heat to a simmer and let cook about 30 minutes. Remove the chicken and allow it to cool.

When you can handle the chicken, remove the meat from the bones. Return chicken to the pot along with the parsnip mixture. Cook another 5 minutes and then taste, adjusting seasoning as needed. When yummy, add rice and cook until tender, about 15 minutes, adding more water or broth if needed. Just before serving, remove a cup of soup, stir the yogurt or sour cream into it, then return to the pot and stir to combine. (This technique prevents the dairy from curdling.)

CHEESY CHOWDER

This is a nice, hearty soup for a chilly night. Add the I Yam What I Yam Sweet Potato Corn Bread (page 32) and you've got a meal.

MAKES 4 SERVINGS

One 6-inch piece reduced-fat kielbasa, sliced (or cut smaller for young children)

1 medium onion, chopped

2 cloves garlic, chopped

2 carrots, thinly sliced

4 cups chicken broth

1 tablespoon Dijon mustard

$^1/_2$ cup grated Cheddar cheese

Heat a large saucepan over medium-high heat. Use just enough oil to coat the pan. Add the kielbasa and let brown. Remove from the pan and drain any excess fat. Add the onions and let cook about 3 minutes or until just starting to turn golden. Add the garlic and let cook another minute, making sure the garlic doesn't burn. Add the carrots, half the broth, and season with salt. Let cook about 10 minutes or until carrots are tender.

Transfer broth and vegetables to the blender and add remaining chicken broth and Dijon mustard. Puree until smooth and return to the pan along with the kielbasa. Bring to a boil, then reduce heat and simmer for 5 minutes. Ladle soup into bowls and top with cheese. Blame the major food company that produced your cheese for any unmelted cheese in the bowls.

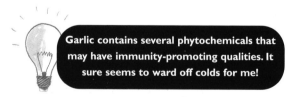

Garlic contains several phytochemicals that may have immunity-promoting qualities. It sure seems to ward off colds for me!

THAI BUTTERNUT SQUASH AND SHRIMP SOUP

I offer this under the heading You Never Know; if you had to eat "kid" food every night you might lose your mind. I have a niece who loves Thai coconut soup and find she'll eat anything floating in coconut milk. If yours only pull out the shrimp and leave the soup, they will still be getting a whisper of vitamin A, and I'm willing to count that a victory.

MAKES 4 SERVINGS

One 15-ounce can lite coconut milk

1 cup chicken broth

One 10-ounce box butternut squash puree, defrosted

1 teaspoon coriander

1 teaspoon cumin powder

Juice of 1 lime

1 tablespoon brown sugar or honey

1 tablespoon soy sauce or fish sauce if your pantry is "happening"

14 medium shrimp, cooked or raw

Chopped cilantro for garnish, optional

Heat a large saucepan over medium-high heat. Combine the coconut milk, broth, and squash. Whisk together until smooth and season with salt. Add the coriander, cumin, lime juice, brown sugar or honey, and soy or fish sauce, then stir again. Bring to a boil, then reduce heat and simmer for 5 minutes. Taste and adjust seasoning—need more coriander, honey, lime, or soy sauce? When yummy, add the shrimp. If using raw shrimp, let cook about 2 minutes, then remove from heat and serve. If using cooked shrimp, remove immediately from the heat. Serve with cilantro, if using.

Not only do frozen vegetables tend to retain their nutrients, they are also a bargain compared to many fresh vegetables. Have a good look at all the options in your market.

VALENTINE CHICKEN SOUP

If you make the bell pepper hearts in the morning, you can have this ready in 3 minutes flat. What's not to love?

MAKES 2 SERVINGS

¹/₂ red bell pepper

I can favorite chicken soup

Prep the pepper by cutting off the top and bottom, and by removing the seeds and the white "ribs." Slit and lay the pepper flat, skin side down, on a cutting board. Using a heart cookie cutter, ¹/₂ inch or smaller in diameter, cut out 6 to 12 tiny hearts.

Prepare the soup according to the directions on the package. Stir in the hearts and let them heat through or simmer for a few minutes to soften if your family members prefer their vegetables on the tender side.

If you purchased a whole set of mini cookie cutters, use the other cutters to add fun-shaped vegetables to any soup.

LEEK AND POTATO SOUP

Leeks are in the same family as garlic and onions. This family is rich in phytochemicals and antioxidants and a bunch of other big words that seem to translate into improved quality of life. Make this with fresh thyme for best results.

MAKES 4 SERVINGS

2 leeks, white part only (save those tops for vegetable broth)

1 tablespoon butter

1 clove garlic, chopped

4 cups chicken broth

1 pound Idaho potatoes, peeled and cut into $^1/_2$-inch pieces

6 sprigs fresh thyme leaves or 1 teaspoon dried thyme

$^1/_4$ cup reduced-fat sour cream or yogurt

Slice leeks in half lengthwise and remove the root. Chop into 1-inch pieces and place in a large bowl filled with tepid water, separating the layers. Let soak 10 minutes, then remove from the bowl.

Heat a large saucepan over medium heat. Add the butter and the leeks and cook about 5 minutes or until tender. Add the garlic and cook another minute. Add the chicken broth, potatoes, and thyme, then bring to a simmer and cook about 8 minutes or until potatoes are tender. Remove from heat and allow to cool slightly (hot soup will try to escape the blender, potentially causing a mess or injury). Place in blender in batches and puree until smooth, then return to pan. Bring to a simmer and taste, adjusting seasoning as needed. Ladle soup into bowls and place a dollop of sour cream or yogurt on top.

Thyme is the perfect beginner herb. It goes with almost everything, is hard to overdo, and will last a very long time in the crisper drawer. Even when dried out, its flavor beats that of the stuff in a spice jar.

BEEF AND VEGGIE STARS SOUP

This simple soup tastes great; and even if you can get only one star into them, your family will always think fondly of you for going to the trouble to make it for them.

MAKES 4 SERVINGS

2 medium carrots, peeled and cut into $^1/_8$-inch planks

2 parsnips, peeled and cut into $^1/_8$-inch planks

1 medium onion, finely chopped

1 stalk celery, finely chopped

$^1/_2$ pound round steak, cut into $^1/_2$-inch cubes

4 cups beef, chicken, or vegetable broth

1 bay leaf

Using a $^1/_2$-inch star cookie cutter, cut carrots and parsnips into stars. Reserve scraps for another pot of soup or vegetable broth.

Heat a soup pot on medium-high heat. Add just enough oil to coat the bottom of the pan, then add the onion and celery, and cook until golden. Add the beef and brown, stirring a few times. Add the broth and bay leaf, season with salt, and bring to a boil. Reduce heat to a simmer and cook about 10 minutes. Add the vegetable stars and cook another 10 minutes. Taste and adjust seasoning, then serve while singing a song about stars.

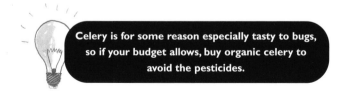

Celery is for some reason especially tasty to bugs, so if your budget allows, buy organic celery to avoid the pesticides.

2-MINUTE BASIL ZUCCHINI SOUP

This is the soup you serve when it is nine thousand degrees outside and eight thousand degrees in your kitchen. It's cool, creamy, and refreshing with a side order of nutrients, oh yeah!

MAKES 4 SERVINGS

2 cups chicken broth

1 cup buttermilk

2 small to medium zucchini, cut into 1-inch pieces

10–20 basil leaves or 1–2 tablespoons pesto

Put everything in the blender and puree until smooth. Chill for one hour or serve immediately. (If you wait an hour, though, it's not really 2-minute soup, is it?)

When "they" say you need 5–7 servings a day of fruits and vegetables, don't panic. Have a look at your 1/2-cup measure. Not so big, right? That's one serving. For kids, the serving size is even smaller. Because one of our problems is portion control, we tend to think we couldn't possibly eat that many servings of fruits and vegetables a day, but we can with a little planning. So, exhale and keep plugging away. Every little bit helps…every little bit helps…every little bit helps.

JERUSALEM ARTICHOKE CHICKEN NOODLE SOUP

Also known as sunchokes, these knobby fellas are a good source of vitamin C, thiamin, iron, and fiber. They have a slightly sweet, nutty flavor. Look for ones with smooth unblemished skin in the market and just scrub them—the skin is where the iron is. They oxidize quickly, so cut them just before cooking.

MAKES 4–6 SERVINGS

1 medium onion, chopped

2–4 cloves garlic, chopped

4 cups chicken or vegetable broth

1 carrot, thinly sliced

1 Jerusalem artichoke, scrubbed and tough knobs removed

$1/4$ pound spaghetti noodles, broken into 1- to 2-inch pieces

Juice of $1/2$ lemon or 1 teaspoon rice vinegar

Heat a soup pot over medium-high heat. Use just enough oil to coat the bottom of the pan, then add the onion and sauté until softened. Add the garlic and cook another minute, making sure the garlic doesn't burn. Add the chicken broth and carrots to the pot. Cut the Jerusalem artichoke into $1/2$-inch pieces and add to the pot. Bring to a boil, reduce the heat to a simmer, and cook for about 15 minutes or until the Jerusalem artichoke is tender. Remove from the heat and cool slightly (hot soup will try to escape the blender, potentially causing a mess or injury). Place into the blender and puree until smooth. You may have to puree in batches, depending on the size of your blender.

Return mixture to the pot over medium-high heat, and bring to a boil. Add spaghetti and lemon juice or vinegar and stir. Let cook about 10–12 minutes or until spaghetti is "al dente," then taste and adjust seasoning, and ladle away.

The Jerusalem artichoke is neither an artichoke nor from Jerusalem. It is the root of a variety of sunflower, which is why they are also known as sunchokes.

CLEAN OUT THE FRIDGE SOUP

Some of the best pots of soup I've ever made I'll never have again because I won't have the same mix of vegetables. Use any of the veggies lying around: frozen, fresh, a little past their prime, a nub of tomato or onion—you name it! I like the middle part of broccoli and asparagus stems in this soup. This is a great dish in which to practice the art of seasoning, so be brave and have fun!

MAKES 6–10 SERVINGS

Selection of vegetables
Chicken broth and water, as needed
1–2 medium onions, finely chopped
2–5 cloves garlic, finely chopped
Other things from the fridge

Place vegetable pieces in a pot with enough chicken broth and water to cover, and season with salt. Let the veggies simmer until they're tender, about 20 minutes. Let the soup cool briefly (hot soup will try to escape the blender, potentially causing a mess or injury), transfer to the blender, and puree until smooth. Don't overfill the blender—puree in batches if necessary.

Return the pot to medium-high heat. Use just enough oil to coat the bottom of the pot and then add the onions. Cook until they start to turn golden, then add the garlic and cook another 30 seconds. Return the pureed veggies to the pot and stir well. Add any little hunks of chicken or meat, especially if it's smoky—I have used pepperoni, ham, or even cold cuts. Add a little salt and other favorite seasonings (I think thyme is great in soup) and let simmer about 5 minutes. If you would like a chunkier soup you can add additional chopped vegetables at this point. Taste your soup and see what you think. Does it need salt, sugar, lemon juice, or vinegar? How about a squirt of ketchup? Salsa? Always start with a small amount of whatever you're adding since you can always add more, but once it's in, it's in!

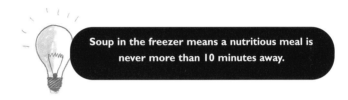

Soup in the freezer means a nutritious meal is never more than 10 minutes away.

SIDE
DISHES

COVERT CAULIFLOWER
MASHED POTATOES

Cauliflower has many of the virtues of broccoli with the distinct advantage of being white! This is a truly painless way to get a veggie into your family's tummies, and honestly, nobody ever detects it. Start bumping up the amount of cauliflower after making it a couple of times.

MAKES 4 SERVINGS

1 pound Idaho potatoes, peeled and cut into 2-inch pieces

2 cloves garlic, halved

¹/₄ head cauliflower, cut into florets, or 5 ounces (¹/₂ box) of frozen, defrosted

2 tablespoons butter

¹/₂ cup milk or buttermilk

Fill a medium saucepan with just enough cold water to cover the potatoes. Add the garlic and a couple pinches of salt. Bring to a boil, then reduce heat and simmer until potatoes are tender, about 15 minutes total.

When potatoes are about half cooked, at about 8 minutes, add cauliflower and cook another 7 minutes. When veggies are tender, drain them. Using a ricer, hand mixer, or masher (a ricer works best), mash well. Stir in butter and milk or buttermilk, and season with salt and pepper. Taste and adjust seasoning.

> Mashed potatoes freeze well, so make a double batch and freeze half to have on hand. The potatoes will need to be stirred for uniform consistency, since freezing causes some separation.

24-CARAT CHEESY MASHED POTATOES

This dish is a treasure. The cheese perfectly explains the color and makes the flavor irresistible. Yukon Gold is a variety of potato with a golden color and slightly creamy texture. Many people find that because of the creaminess they tend to use less butter and milk when making mashed potatoes. If Yukon Gold is unavailable, use Idaho potatoes.

MAKES 4 SERVINGS

1 pound Yukon Gold potatoes, peeled and cut into 2-inch pieces

1 carrot, peeled and thinly sliced

2 tablespoons grated Parmesan cheese

1 ounce Cheddar cheese, grated

1 tablespoon butter

1/2 cup milk or buttermilk

Combine the potatoes, carrots, and a couple pinches of salt in a medium saucepan and cover with cold water. Bring to a boil, then reduce heat and let simmer until veggies are tender, about 15 minutes.

Drain potatoes and carrots. Using a ricer, hand mixer, or masher (a ricer works best), mash until smooth. Stir in both cheeses, butter, and milk or buttermilk, then season with salt and pepper. Taste and adjust seasoning. Notice how exceptionally satisfied you feel after dinner.

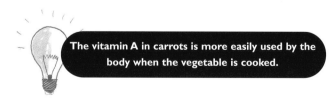

The vitamin A in carrots is more easily used by the body when the vegetable is cooked.

CAULIFLOWER AND POTATOES AU GRATIN

You can't help but love anything with an *au Gratin* at the end of the name. This is a heart-healthy version that contains our little secret ingredient—more to love! Potatoes have very little flavor if under-seasoned, so be a bit braver with the salt in this recipe.

MAKES 4 SERVINGS

2 tablespoons butter, divided

2 medium Idaho potatoes

1/3 head cauliflower

1/2 cup grated Parmesan cheese

1/4 cup grated mozzarella cheese

3 cloves garlic, finely chopped

I cup chicken broth

1/4 cup buttermilk

Preheat the oven to 425°F. Butter a 9 × 9 baking dish.

Slice the potatoes thinly (a mandoline will work best). Grate the cauliflower using the smallest holes on the grater. Place 1/3 of the potatoes in the bottom of the baking dish, followed by 1/3 of the cauliflower. Season with salt and sprinkle with 1/3 of each of the cheeses and 1/3 of the garlic. Top with dots of butter and repeat two more times with remaining vegetables, cheese, garlic, and butter. Bring broth to a boil either on the stove-top or in the microwave. Pour over the top of the vegetables and then drizzle on the buttermilk. Bake for 45 minutes or until the vegetables are tender and the top is golden brown. You can check by inserting a paring knife into the center. Remove from the oven and let rest for 5 minutes before serving.

Gratin in French refers to any dish topped with cheese, bread crumbs, and butter, and cooked until crispy and golden. Try making any vegetable you like this way for a slightly dressy side dish.

CONFETTI COUSCOUS

The secret to this pretty dish is cutting everything into a tiny dice. I find that couscous is fluffiest when made with a pat of butter rather than olive oil—please, forgive me, traditionalists! It's nice at room temperature too, so make it for your next buffet dinner or potluck. Feel free to add just about any vegetable you...or they...like.

MAKES 4 SERVINGS

1 cup vegetable or chicken broth

1 tablespoon butter

1 cup couscous (make me happy, and make it whole wheat)

$1/2$ red bell pepper, cut into $1/4$-inch pieces

$1/2$ yellow bell pepper, cut into $1/4$-inch pieces

$1/2$ green bell pepper, cut into $1/4$-inch pieces

6 dried apricots, cut into $1/4$-inch pieces

$1/4$ cup dried cranberries (unsweetened)

Heat a medium saucepan over medium-high heat with the broth and the butter. Season with salt and bring to a boil. When boiling, remove from heat, stir in remaining ingredients, and cover. Let stand 5 minutes. Fluff with a fork and enjoy.

Couscous, a Moroccan dish, was originally made by rubbing dough through the holes of a sieve. It was then steamed in a special vessel called a *couscoussière*. For getting dinner on the table quickly, I prefer my saucepan!

EGYPTIAN SPINACH

I'm showing my optimistic side. This is a Bite Club recipe (page 9). Perhaps you can lure them into trying this dish when they study Egypt in school, or after you find them an interesting book about King Tut at the library, whatever it takes. This is by far the tastiest spinach dish I know.

2 tablespoons butter

1 medium onion, finely chopped

2 plum tomatoes, chopped

1 teaspoon coriander

2 cloves garlic, chopped

One 10-ounce box frozen spinach, defrosted

$^1/_2$–$^3/_4$ cup chicken broth

1 can garbanzo beans, drained

Juice of 1 lemon

Heat a saucepan over medium-high heat. Add the butter and onions, and cook until just starting to turn golden, about 3 minutes. Add the tomatoes, coriander, and garlic and cook until tomatoes are softened, about 5 minutes. Add spinach and chicken broth, then season with salt and stir well. Bring to a boil, then reduce heat and let simmer 5 minutes. Add garbanzo beans and lemon juice, and then cook another minute. Taste and adjust seasoning. Serve in small bowls or over rice.

Lutein is an antioxidant that seems to benefit eyes, skin, and cardiovascular health. It is found in dark, green leafy vegetables (like spinach), fruit, corn, and egg yolks.

PARSNIP PANCAKES WITH APPLESAUCE AND SOUR CREAM

This would make a nice meatless main course. Your family will probably eat anything topped with applesauce and sour cream, and they will love these.

MAKES 4 SERVINGS

1 ½ pounds parsnips, peeled
½ medium onion
1 egg, lightly beaten
¼ cup all-purpose flour
A few grates of nutmeg
Applesauce, as needed
Reduced-fat sour cream, as needed

Place parsnips in a saucepan with a little water and steam for 3 minutes. Let cool slightly.

In a food processor fitted with the shredding blade or with a hand grater, shred the parsnips and the onion. Transfer both to a mixing bowl and add the egg, flour, and nutmeg, then season with salt. Stir together.

Line a plate or sheet pan with paper towels. Heat a skillet with ¼ inch of oil over medium heat. When oil is hot (test it with a small amount of the mixture), fry a tiny patty of mixture and taste, adjusting seasoning if needed. Remove pan from heat and form 8 patties from remaining mixture. Return pan to the heat and, when hot, fry patties until golden brown. Remove patties to paper towels. You may hold them at this point for up to 1 hour and then reheat in a 300°F oven for 5–7 minutes. Top with applesauce and sour cream.

Nutmeg is one of those slightly mysterious spices. It gives dishes a little something extra that you can't define but really makes a difference. Try to include it when called for and always grate your own as you use it. Use a microplaner or the funny, small "outie" holes on your grater. Unlike grated nutmeg, whole nutmeg lasts practically forever.

BROCCOLI BOBS

This is simply the truly tasty Try It, You'll Like It: Parmesan Broccoli Dip (page 22) transformed into a side dish with the addition of eggs. Presto change-o!

MAKES 4 SERVINGS

1 recipe Try It, You'll Like It: Parmesan Broccoli Dip (page 22)
2 large eggs, lightly beaten

Preheat the oven to 350°F. Butter or spray four ramekins, custard cups, or cups in a muffin tin.

Combine the dip and eggs in a medium bowl and stir well. Divide mixture between ramekins, custard cups, or the muffin tin cups. Bake for about 20 minutes or until mixture is set and just starting to brown. Let cool a few minutes, then run a sharp paring knife around the edges and invert onto a plate. Serve warm.

Broccoli is rich in vitamins **A** and **C** and contains several phytochemicals that promote health and prevent disease.

COOLEST CAULIFLOWER EVER

This is an all-visual sneak. You will be serving two different purees in a yin-yang motif. Even if the family isn't into martial arts or doesn't support a green and purple sports team, this dish is just too eye-popping not to at least taste. This is a bit labor intensive so make a double batch and freeze half.

MAKES 4 SERVINGS

$^1/_4$ **head purple cauliflower**

$^1/_4$ **head broccoflower (a lime green cross between cauliflower and broccoli)**

2 cloves garlic, divided

$^1/_2$ **cup milk or buttermilk, divided**

2 tablespoons butter, divided

Steam the cauliflower and broccoflower in a medium saucepan with a little water until tender, about 8 minutes.

Place the purple cauliflower in the blender with 1 clove of garlic and half the milk or buttermilk, then season with salt. Puree until smooth, then remove to a small saucepan over low heat and stir in 1 tablespoon of butter. Taste and adjust seasoning and cook about 2 minutes.

Rinse out the blender and repeat as above with the steamed broccoflower and remaining ingredients.

To serve, spoon a little purple cauliflower mash onto the plate and swirl a little tail over the top. Nestle a spoonful of the broccoflower puree under the tail and swirl a little tail of broccoflower under the purple cauliflower puree in a yin-yang design. Deliver to the table with a resounding "Hyee ya!"

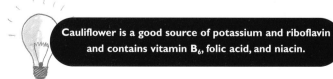

Cauliflower is a good source of potassium and riboflavin and contains vitamin B$_6$, folic acid, and niacin.

PARSNIPS POSING AS PURPLE MASHED POTATOES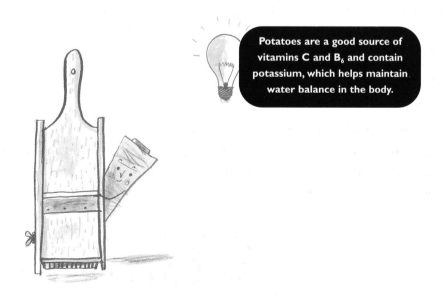

Most markets will have purple potatoes at some point during the year. The color holds when the potatoes are cooked, making for a lovely batch of colorful spuds.

MAKES 4 SERVINGS

1 pound purple Peruvian new potatoes, scrubbed and quartered

2 cloves garlic, halved

2 medium parsnips, peeled and thinly sliced

2 tablespoons butter

$^{1}/_{2}$ cup milk or buttermilk

Fill a medium saucepan with cold water and add the potatoes, garlic, parsnips, and a couple pinches of salt. Bring to a boil, then reduce heat and let simmer until potatoes are tender, about 15 minutes. Drain, then using a ricer, hand mixer, or masher (a ricer works best), mash well. Stir in butter and milk or buttermilk, and season with salt. Taste and adjust seasoning. Discuss alliteration over dinner.

> Potatoes are a good source of vitamins **C** and **B**$_6$ and contain potassium, which helps maintain water balance in the body.

MARINATED KALE

While this is absolutely a Bite Club recipe (page 9), the sweetness of the dressing makes it quite tasty. It might take eight bites but...kale is an excellent source of vitamins A and C and a good source of calcium, iron, and B$_6$, hence my optimism. Maybe your children don't realize that your family is a charter member of the Bite Club and that your good standing could be in jeopardy if they don't eat up.

MAKES 6 SERVINGS

1 bunch kale, large stems removed

3 tablespoons rice vinegar

2–3 tablespoons olive oil

2 teaspoons Dijon mustard

1–2 tablespoons soy sauce

2 teaspoons finely minced garlic

2–3 tablespoons honey

Roll kale leaves two at a time like a cigar and cut into ribbons. You may want to cut the ribbons if they seem too long. Place in a large bowl.

In a small bowl, whisk together remaining ingredients and taste, adjusting seasoning as needed. Pour over kale and toss to coat. Refrigerate overnight, tossing once if you think of it.

Kale is sweetest when fresh, so prepare it soon after purchase for best flavor.

BAKED CAULIFLOWER

The secret to this one is getting your family to try it. Golden brown on top and creamy inside, it does tempt. It is not strictly heart healthy, but if it will get them to realize they like cauliflower, it will be worth it a few times a year.

MAKES 4–6 SERVINGS

1 head cauliflower, cut into florets

6 tablespoons butter

$^1/_2$ medium onion, finely chopped

2 tablespoons all-purpose flour (how 'bout whole wheat or oat flour?)

1 cup buttermilk

$^1/_2$ cup chicken broth

$^1/_2$ cup bread crumbs

$^1/_2$ cup grated Parmesan cheese

Preheat the oven to 350°F. Butter or spray a 9 × 9 inch baking dish.

Lay cauliflower in the bottom of the baking dish. Season with salt.

In a skillet over medium heat, sauté the butter and onions until softened, about 2 minutes. Sprinkle the flour over the onions and combine. Cook about 2 minutes, stirring constantly. Stir in the buttermilk and the chicken broth and bring to a boil. Remove from heat and season with salt. Pour over the cauliflower.

In a small bowl, mix together the bread crumbs and the Parmesan cheese, then sprinkle over the top of the cauliflower. Bake for 30–40 minutes or until golden and bubbly.

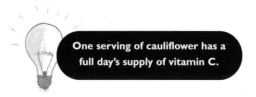

One serving of cauliflower has a full day's supply of vitamin C.

CORN PUDDING WITH CARAMELIZED ONIONS AND SQUASH

I love the creaminess of this savory custard, and so will the kids. This would be great on a holiday table or as a special dish for guests. The squash will resemble corn if you are able to cut it small enough. Holiday doesn't mean taking a day off from nutrition!

MAKES 6 SERVINGS

1 medium onion, finely chopped

2 teaspoons sugar

1 small yellow squash, finely chopped

2 cups frozen corn, defrosted, divided

1 1/2 cups half-and-half

2 large eggs

A few grates of nutmeg

Chopped parsley or chives (if they won't offend anyone)

Heat a skillet over medium-high heat. Use just enough oil to coat the bottom of the pan, then add the onion and cook, stirring occasionally, for 3 minutes. Add the sugar, season with salt, and continue to cook another minute. Add the squash and cook until both are golden. Remove from heat and reserve.

Preheat the oven to 325°F. Put a saucepan of water on to boil. Butter or spray a 9 × 9 inch baking dish.

In the blender, combine 1 cup corn, half-and-half, eggs, and nutmeg, and season with salt. Puree until smooth. Pour into a mixing bowl and add the reserved onion and squash, the remaining corn, and parsley or chives if using. Pour into prepared baking dish.

Place baking dish into a slightly larger baking dish or small roasting pan, and place on the center rack in the oven. Pour boiling water around the outside of the smaller baking dish (the water will protect the eggs during baking). Bake 90 minutes or until the center is set but still soft. Remove from the oven and let rest 10–15 minutes before serving.

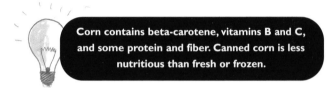

Corn contains beta-carotene, vitamins B and C, and some protein and fiber. Canned corn is less nutritious than fresh or frozen.

HALLOWEEN MASHED POTATOES

The name is the only sneaky thing here. Of course, you could make some Halloween cupcakes for dessert and be sure they see the orange food coloring going into the frosting....

2 Idaho potatoes, peeled and cut into 1-inch pieces

2 medium sweet potatoes or yams, peeled and cut into 1-inch pieces

2 tablespoons butter

3–4 tablespoons milk or buttermilk

Put both kinds of potatoes and a generous pinch of salt into a saucepan, cover with water, and place over medium-high heat. Bring to a boil and cook about 10 minutes or until the potatoes are tender, then drain. Using a ricer, hand mixer, or masher (a ricer works best), mash well. Stir in butter and milk or buttermilk, then season with salt. Taste and adjust seasoning. Serve wearing a funny nose and a fake mole.

 Sweet potatoes are native to the Americas. The remains of twenty-thousand-year-old sweet potatoes have been found in caves in Peru. They became a staple for early settlers who cultivated them in the American colonies and are now cultivated in many parts of the world.

CHICORY HIDING IN THE SALAD

You can tuck any leafy green in your usual salad, but I chose chicory because it's a good source of calcium; magnesium; riboflavin; potassium; folate; vitamins A, B_6, and C; and fiber. Does it get any better?

MAKES 4 SERVINGS

1 bag of family-favorite "ready salad"

$^1/_4$ head chicory, washed and spun or blotted dry

Salad dressing of choice (I choose the Hidden Veggie Ranch Dressing, page 16)

Toss greens with dressing and serve.

You hear again and again that you need to be eating leafy greens more often. Have a look at all the varieties available in the bagged salad section of your market and try a new one on your family from time to time. They might just go for it the eighth...or twelfth...time you ask.

VEGETABLE "NOODLES" WITH PARMESAN CHEESE

We're taking the novelty approach here. Since slurping "basketti" is good messy fun, these "noodles" might fly. The bright colors help too. You will need a mandoline (page 10) to make this dish. If one of the veggies just won't do in your house, double up on another. Even those who don't generally like cooked carrots enjoy them in this guise. To make it more of a main course, add rotisserie chicken or any cooked protein.

MAKES 4 SERVINGS

1 tablespoon butter

2–4 tablespoons chicken or vegetable broth

2 medium carrots, sliced lengthwise with the medium comb blade

2 medium zucchini, sliced lengthwise with the medium comb blade

2 medium yellow squash, sliced lengthwise with the medium comb blade

4 tablespoons grated Parmesan cheese

Heat a large skillet over medium heat. Add the butter and swirl to coat the bottom of the pan. Add 2 tablespoons of the broth and the carrots, then season with salt. Cook about 3 minutes, add the zucchini and squash, then season with salt and toss gently. Cook another minute, adding more broth if needed, then plate, top with Parmesan, and serve.

All three of these vegetables can be eaten raw, so try making a crunchy "noodle" salad with them and serve with a favorite dressing.

SIMPLY DELICIOUS
SUGAR SNAP PEAS

**Sing the title to the tune of "Jimmy Crack Corn" if you didn't pick
up on it already. To make this very obvious green vegetable more of
an adventure, pop open the pods and show your kids the tiny peas
inside. In addition, you can explain that this is where the expression
"as cozy as two peas in a pod" came from. And, as I sang in the
recipe title, if they don't eat them you will, because they are so
sweet and tasty.**

MAKES 4 SERVINGS

4 fistfuls sugar snap peas

2 teaspoons soy sauce

A few drops sesame oil

Heat a large saucepan with well-salted water. When boiling, add snap peas and cook for
1 minute. Drain and toss with soy sauce and sesame oil.

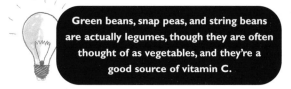

Green beans, snap peas, and string beans
are actually legumes, though they are often
thought of as vegetables, and they're a
good source of vitamin C.

OVEN-FRIED ZUCCHINI STICKS

Everything tastes good deep fried. Unfortunately, it's probably not good for us. Fortunately, we have a tasty compromise in these guys. They taste fried and have a yumola coating of Parmesan, but they won't shorten your life.

MAKES 4 SERVINGS

$1/4$ cup bread crumbs

$1/2$ cup grated Parmesan cheese

2–3 medium zucchini, cut into 3-inch spears

1 egg, lightly beaten

Preheat the oven to 400°F. Line a cookie sheet or a jelly roll pan with foil, shiny side down. Spray or drizzle oil on the foil.

Combine the bread crumbs, Parmesan, and salt in a medium bowl until well mixed.

Dip the zucchini spears into the egg and then into the bread crumb mixture. Lay the spears on the prepared sheet pan. Place in the oven and bake for 5–7 minutes, then turn the spears over and return to the oven for another 5–7 minutes or until golden and crispy. Best served hot.

I like to slice zucchini "chips" and put them out with dips as another way to try and get in those pesky 5–7 servings.

HASHED BRUSSELS SPROUTS

The secret to Brussels sprouts is choosing small ones and blanching them briefly before cooking to remove bitterness. Oh, and in this recipe, we're going to shred them into oblivion and add a little bacon, because they're Brussels sprouts! You could try "forgetting" the sour cream after they've enjoyed this a few times.

1 pint (about 10 ounces) Brussels sprouts, stems trimmed

$^{1}/_{4}$ cup chicken broth

4 strips bacon (regular or turkey), chopped

$^{1}/_{2}$ medium onion, finely chopped

2 cloves garlic, finely chopped

2–3 tablespoons reduced-fat sour cream

Bring a saucepan of well-salted water to a boil. Add the Brussels sprouts and cook 2 minutes. Drain, then cover with cold water for 5 minutes and drain again.

Quarter the Brussels sprouts and place in the food processor. Pulse several times until evenly chopped. After removing any large pieces of stem, place in a bowl and toss with the chicken broth.

Heat a skillet over medium-high heat, cook the bacon until crispy, and remove to paper towels to drain. Discard any excess fat in the pan and add the onion. Let cook about 3 minutes, then add the garlic and cook another 30 seconds. Add the Brussels sprouts and broth, season with salt, and cook about 3 minutes. Remove from heat, stir in sour cream, then sprinkle bacon over the top before serving.

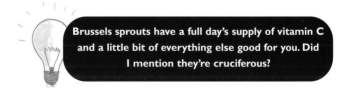

Brussels sprouts have a full day's supply of vitamin C and a little bit of everything else good for you. Did I mention they're cruciferous?

WHITE ASPARAGUS BREAD PUDDING MUFFINS

These are like popovers, but they don't really pop (I was tempted to call them popunders). They make a nice alternative to the usual brunch fare and can be frozen. Just defrost in the fridge overnight and warm in a 300°F oven for about 10 minutes.

MAKES 8 MUFFINS

$1/2$ pound whole wheat rolls or other bread

One 7- or 8-ounce jar (not can) white asparagus, drained

2 large eggs

4 ounces Swiss or other firm cheese, grated

$1/2$ cup buttermilk

Preheat the oven to 350°F. Spray a muffin tin or line it with eight muffin papers.

In a large mixing bowl, rip the rolls into 1-inch pieces. Cut the asparagus into $1/2$- inch pieces and toss with the bread. Lightly beat the eggs, cheese, and buttermilk together, then season with salt. Pour over the bread mixture and fold together. Spoon the mixture into the prepared tin. Bake for 20–25 minutes or until eggs appear cooked and golden brown.

White asparagus is identical to green but has been grown with soil mounded around it to prevent it from turning green.

SPAGHETTI SQUASH

Spaghetti squash was all the rage in the 1980s. I'm not sure if a diet craze made it popular or just the novelty of it, but it has a mild flavor that everyone seems to like. Just call it noodles and you aren't lying. Turn this into a main course by adding a traditional meat sauce or cooked chicken. Because it's all vegetable, don't feel guilty about the butter.

MAKES 4–6 SERVINGS

1 medium spaghetti squash (about 3 pounds)

1 medium onion, chopped

2 cloves garlic, finely chopped

$\frac{1}{2}$ cup chicken broth

4 tablespoons butter

1 cup frozen peas, defrosted (ya gotta give 'em something to pick out)

$\frac{1}{2}$ red bell pepper, cut into $\frac{1}{4}$-inch pieces

4–6 tablespoons grated Parmesan cheese

Preheat the oven to 350°F.

With a paring knife, prick the skin of the squash all over. Place in a baking dish or on a sheet pan and bake for 1 hour.

Heat a small skillet over medium-high heat. Add just enough oil to coat the bottom of the pan, then add the onions. Cook about 3 minutes, then add the garlic and cook another minute, making sure the garlic doesn't burn. Add the chicken broth, butter, and peas and bring to a simmer. Cook 3 minutes. Then add the peppers and remove from heat.

When the squash is done, let it cool slightly, then slice in half lengthwise. Using a fork, scrape the "spaghetti" out and into a serving bowl, separating the strands if needed. Gently reheat the sauce if it has cooled, and pour over the squash. Toss lightly and top with Parmesan.

WE MET THE FARMER WHO GREW THE STIR-FRIED RAMPS

Of all the foods you can get only in season—and there are fewer and fewer every year—ramps are my all-time favorite. They are slightly sweet wild leeks with a mellow onion flavor. They grow from the Carolinas up to Canada and are harvested in the spring. Ramps can be purchased online, but I'm picturing a family trip to the farmer's market where you find that ramps have appeared. You are euphoric and explain how exciting it is that it's ramp season. You then exclaim, "Ramp Stir-Fry tonight!" The worst-case scenario is that they won't even take a bite, and you can eat all of them yourself. I guarantee that the look on your face when you take your first bite will get them to try them someday and lament all the years of ramps they missed out on.

3 bunches of ramps, about $^1/_2$ pound
1 tablespoon canola or grape seed oil
1 tablespoon butter

Soak the roots of the ramps in a bowl of tepid water for a few minutes. Remove and soak again if needed. Drain, rinse the bowl, then refill with tepid water and dip the tops of the ramps in. Slosh them around a bit and remove. Repeat if needed. Using a paper towel, gently wipe down the bulbs. Then remove roots with a paring knife.

Cut the bulbs and the red part of the stems off and place together. Cut the leafy green tops into 1-inch pieces and put aside separately.

Heat a large skillet over medium-high heat. Add the oil and swirl around, then add the butter. Add the bulb portions of the ramps and season with salt. Toss several times and cook about 2 minutes. Add the leaves, season with a little more salt, and toss several more times, then serve. I don't have to ask you to make yummy sounds with your first bite, you just will on your own!

MAIN

COURSES

SALMON CAKES WITH CARROTS

The carrot stowaways disappear into the background of the salmon. The only complaint you'll get with these will be "Arrgh, they're all gone!" Try it with other fish if your family doesn't care for salmon.

MAKES 4 SERVINGS

3 fillets of salmon (about $^3/_4$ of a pound total)

2 medium carrots, thinly sliced

$^1/_4$ cup I Call It Dreamy: Creamy Sandwich Spread (page 18)

Juice of I lemon

I stalk celery, finely chopped

2 teaspoons fresh or dried dill

I tablespoon Dijon mustard

I egg, lightly beaten

$^1/_2$ cup bread crumbs

Feeling Better 'bout Fish Sticks: Rockin' Tartar Sauce (page 19)

In the bowl of the food processor, place the salmon and pulse several times until the fish is evenly chopped, but not mush. Remove fish from food processor to a medium mixing bowl. Now, place the carrots, the sandwich spread, and the lemon juice in the food processor. Process until carrots are uniformly tiny, then transfer to the bowl with the fish. Add the celery, dill, mustard, egg, and bread crumbs to the mixing bowl and season with salt, then fold together. You may want to fry up a small piece to taste and then adjust the seasoning as needed. The mixture can be frozen at this point.

Form eight patties with the mixture. Line a plate with paper towels. Heat a skillet with about $^1/_4$ inch of oil in the bottom. When the oil is hot, fry the patties until deep golden brown, then remove to the towel-lined plate. They can be made 1 hour ahead and reheated in a 350°F oven for 5–8 minutes. Serve with plenty of tartar sauce.

CARROTY FRIDAY NIGHT TACOS

While inhaling these they'll be getting a harmless dose of beta-carotene. The taco seasoning allows the carrots to blend in beautifully. You could even try giving broccoli the same treatment after making this recipe a few times. I don't generally condone seasoning mixes, but in this case tacos taste just like tacos and it's Friday night—you're pooped.

MAKES 4–6 SERVINGS

2 medium carrots, peeled and thinly sliced

1 envelope taco seasoning

³/₄ cup water

1 pound lean ground beef or turkey

Twelve 6-inch tortillas or taco shells

Assorted toppings: shredded cheese, lettuce, chopped tomatoes

Reduced-fat sour cream

Salsa

Place carrots in blender with taco seasoning and water, then puree until only tiny bits remain. Remove any telltale chunks.

Heat a large skillet over medium-high heat. When pan is hot, add meat (for ground turkey you might need a bit of oil in the pan) and brown. Well-cooked meat is important. When meat is evenly browned, drain any fat from the pan, add carrot mixture, and stir well. Reduce heat and let simmer about 5 minutes. Remove from heat.

Place meat in taco shell or tortillas and top with cheese before anyone looks too closely. Begging them to have lettuce and tomato will distract them, and if asked: "Hmm, must be some kind of seasoning" should allay any suspicions.

For a shot of beta-carotene in any soup, stew, or even a smoothie, simmer a sliced carrot or two with a little water until tender. Puree in the blender until smooth and keep on hand in the freezer to add any time.

LASAGNA WITH PARSNIPS

The parsnips will just about disappear into this dish if sliced thinly. Use a mandoline for the thinnest slices (page 10). Perhaps you don't know that you don't need to boil the noodles first or can use no-boil noodles. When baked covered, the bubbling sauce will cook the noodles just fine.

MAKES 8 SERVINGS

One 26-ounce jar pasta sauce or 2 recipes I Don't Feel the Least Bit Guilty: All-Purpose (Perfectly Smooth) Tomato Carrot Sauce (page 29)

1 pound lasagna noodles

One 16-ounce container part-skim ricotta cheese

2 medium parsnips, thinly sliced

1 pound reduced-fat mozzarella cheese, shredded

¼ cup grated Parmesan cheese

Preheat the oven to 350°F. Spread 1 cup sauce on the bottom of a 9 × 13 baking dish (or two smaller dishes). Top with a layer of noodles. Spread half the ricotta on top of the noodles, followed by half the parsnips and a cup of the mozzarella. Top with a cup of sauce and another layer of noodles. Repeat. Top with remaining sauce and mozzarella cheese and sprinkle on Parmesan cheese.

Bake, covered with foil, for 45–60 minutes or until the center is hot and noodles are tender (check by inserting a paring knife in the center). Remove foil and continue to bake until the top starts to brown, about 15 minutes. Remove from oven and let rest 5 minutes before cutting and serving.

To freeze, cover with plastic wrap and aluminum foil. To prepare, defrost overnight in the refrigerator. Replace plastic wrap with foil and bake as above.

Ricotta is naturally high in calcium. In the making of curds and whey, ricotta (whey) gets more of the calcium than the curds (cottage cheese). I like to eat it with a little jelly swirled in.

PUMPKINY SPAGHETTI WITH MEAT SAUCE

Every little bit helps and this little bit will never be noticed!

MAKES 4 SERVINGS

I pound favorite spaghetti

I pound ground beef or turkey, optional

I jar favorite spaghetti sauce

2–4 tablespoons pumpkin puree

Get your water going for the spaghetti and cook according to the package directions.

Heat a large skillet over medium-high heat. Add the ground beef or turkey (you may need to add a little oil to the pan for ground turkey) if using, brown well, and drain any excess fat from the pan. Add the spaghetti sauce and stir in the pumpkin. Let simmer 10–15 minutes, then serve over cooked spaghetti.

> Never feel guilty about using canned pumpkin. Having gone to the trouble to make a pumpkin pie from a whole pumpkin myself, I can tell you that 100 percent pumpkin in a can is the way to go.

BEEF AND VEGETABLE STEW

A common low-fat technique for thickening is using pureed vegetables. Because of the natural sweetness of the parsnips, this stew is especially kid friendly—even if they do pick out the visible veggies.

MAKES 6 SERVINGS

2 medium parsnips, peeled and thinly sliced

1 1/2 cups beef, chicken, or vegetable broth, divided

1 medium onion, finely chopped

2 cloves garlic, finely chopped

1 pound round steak or sirloin tips, cut into 1-inch pieces

3 sprigs thyme leaves or 1 teaspoon dried thyme

1 bay leaf

2 carrots, sliced

2 medium potatoes, scrubbed and cut into bite-sized pieces

Squirt of ketchup

1 tablespoon all-purpose flour, optional

1 tablespoon butter, optional

Chopped parsley, if it doesn't render it inedible for somebody

Heat a small saucepan with the parsnips and half of the broth. Bring to a boil, then reduce to a simmer. Cook until parsnips are tender, about 8 minutes. Remove from heat and let cool slightly. Then transfer to the blender and puree until smooth. Reserve.

In a large saucepan or soup pot over medium-high heat, use just enough oil to coat the bottom, then add the onions and cook until they start to brown. Add the garlic and cook another 30 seconds. Season the meat with salt and pepper, then add to the pot. Let the meat brown well. Add the remaining broth and stir up all the lovely brown bits from the bottom of the pan. Add thyme, bay leaf, carrots, potatoes, and ketchup, then stir. Season with salt and bring to a boil, then reduce heat and let simmer about 20 minutes. Taste and adjust seasoning. When all is yummy and meat is tender, stir in pureed parsnips. Cook for another 5 minutes and check consistency. If you would like it thicker, mix together the flour and butter using a fork until it is smooth. Whisk in half the butter mixture and cook 3 minutes. Check thickness, adding remaining butter mixture if desired. Dust with parsley if you want.

CAULI-FLOWER CHEESE RAVIOLI

Ravioli aren't hard to make! I just love the idea that when the kids ask what's for dinner you can mutter "cauli" before you answer "flower Cheese ravioli." They might wonder what "Flower Cheese" is, but...You can make Christmas tree ravioli or Halloween ghost ravioli. Overly complicated cutters don't work well. Ravioli can be made ahead and frozen to use on a busy night. Woo-hoo!

MAKES 4 SERVINGS

$^1/_2$ box frozen cauliflower, defrosted

4 ounces ricotta cheese, softened

$^1/_2$ cup grated Parmesan cheese, plus some for sprinkling

$^1/_2$ teaspoon dried thyme or a few sprigs thyme leaves

2 large eggs, divided

8 sheets lasagna dough (8 × 12 inches) or 24 wonton wrappers

Butter as needed

Steam cauliflower in a saucepan with $^1/_2$ inch of water until tender, about 8 minutes. Remove and let cool.

In a medium bowl, combine the ricotta, Parmesan, thyme, and 1 egg, then season with salt. Using the small holes on a grater, grate the cauliflower into the mixture and stir to combine.

In a small bowl, lightly beat the remaining egg with a pinch of salt. Carefully lay out a sheet of pasta. Place tablespoon mounds of mixture 1 inch apart and 1 inch from dough edges. Using a pastry brush or your fingers, brush a small amount of egg around each mound. Top with another sheet of pasta and gently press dough down around each mound, removing air bubbles if possible, so that each mound is well sealed. Cut out mounds with a sharp knife or cookie cutter, cover with plastic wrap, and refrigerate for one hour. Repeat with remaining ingredients. Raviolis can be frozen at this point.

To cook, bring a large pot of salted water to a boil. Gently add the raviolis and cook 3–4 minutes. Top with butter and Parmesan and enjoy.

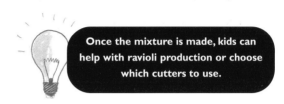

Once the mixture is made, kids can help with ravioli production or choose which cutters to use.

BARBECUED CHICKEN

Some of the best things in life come covered in BBQ sauce, and the little addition here won't change that one bit. Send the leftovers for lunch the next day.

MAKES 8 SERVINGS

2 medium carrots, peeled and thinly sliced

1 bottle family favorite barbecue sauce

8 chicken thighs

Preheat the oven to 350°F.

Place the carrots in a saucepan with ½ inch of water and steam until tender, about 8 minutes. Drain and place in the blender with the barbecue sauce. Puree until smooth.

Place the chicken in a 9 × 9 inch baking dish. Cover with sauce—you might not need all of it. Cover with foil and bake for 30 minutes, then remove the foil and bake another 30 minutes. Have at it!

> **Dark meat has more iron than white meat, so don't feel like you always have to go for the boneless, skinless chicken breast.**

MEDITERRANEAN FISH BAKE WITH FETA

Between the heart-healthy fish, the lycopene-rich cooked toma-toes, and the whisper of cauliflower, this is one virtuous little dish. And! you get to make halibut jokes all night long.

MAKES 4 SERVINGS

1 medium onion, finely chopped

2 cloves garlic, finely chopped

4 plum tomatoes, chopped, or 1 cup tomato sauce

15 leaves fresh basil, chopped (combined immediately with tomatoes)

4 sprigs thyme leaves or $^1/_4$ teaspoon dried thyme

2 tablespoons capers, coarsely chopped, optional

Four 4- to 6-ounce fillets of halibut, sea bass, or any thickish white fish

$^1/_4$ cup feta cheese, crumbled

4 florets cauliflower, grated

$^1/_4$ cup bread crumbs (there is such a thing as whole wheat)

Preheat oven to 375°F. Lightly oil a 9 × 9 baking dish.

In a small bowl, combine the onions, garlic, tomatoes, basil, thyme, and capers if using. Place fillets in baking dish and top with tomato-and-basil mixture. In the same small bowl combine feta, cauliflower, and bread crumbs, then sprinkle over fish. Bake for 15–20 min-utes or until fish is just beginning to flake.

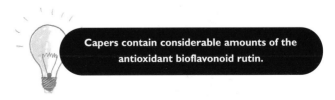

Capers contain considerable amounts of the antioxidant bioflavonoid rutin.

ARTICHOKE AND ROASTED RED PEPPER QUICHE ❄

This crustless quiche is always in my freezer. When not serving it for a last-minute dinner, I cut it into bite-sized squares and serve it as a room temperature hors d'oeuvre that everyone adores (and begs for the recipe). Try sneaking a little spinach into this after it has been well received a few times.

Three 6-ounce jars marinated artichokes, drained
1 bunch scallions, coarsely chopped
4 cloves garlic, chopped
4 sprigs thyme leaves or 1 teaspoon dried thyme
$1/2$ bunch basil leaves or 3 tablespoons pesto
10 large eggs, lightly beaten
1 pound white Cheddar cheese, grated
$1/4$ cup all-purpose flour
1 roasted red bell pepper, chopped, or one 2-ounce jar chopped pimientos

Preheat oven to 350°F. Butter or spray a 9 × 13 inch baking pan, or for extra insurance line it with parchment.

In a food processor, combine artichokes, scallions, garlic, thyme, and basil. Pulse several times until mixture is well chopped and combined but not mushy. Transfer to a large mixing bowl and add eggs, cheese, and flour, then season with about two teaspoons of salt and stir well to combine. Fry up a small amount to check seasoning (you don't want to bake the whole thing and then find out it needed a little more salt).

Pour mixture into pan and smooth out the top. Strew with roasted red peppers or pimientos. Bake for about 30 minutes or until the top is just golden and the center is set—check with a paring knife. Run the paring knife around the edge to loosen, then invert onto a cutting board. To freeze, cut in half and cover each half tightly with 2 layers of plastic wrap. Keeps 2–3 months in the freezer!!

POLKA-DOT CHEESEBURGERS WITH CARROTS AND PARSNIPS

Burgers are one of the great joys in life. With the added nutrition, you will have one more reason to be joyful.

MAKES 4–6 SERVINGS

1 medium parsnip, peeled and thinly sliced

1 medium carrot, peeled and thinly sliced

1 pound ground beef or turkey (a combo maybe?)

1 tablespoon Worcestershire sauce

1 tablespoon ketchup

4 ounces mozzarella cheese, cut into $^1/_4$-inch cubes

Put the parsnips and carrots in a small food processor and pulse several times until no large pieces remain.

Place the beef or turkey in a medium mixing bowl with the carrots, parsnips, Worcestershire sauce, and ketchup and season with salt. Mix gently with your hands, then add the cheese and mix again. Form mixture into patties.

In a skillet over medium-high heat, brown the patties (you may need to add a little oil to the pan for ground turkey). Cook about 5–7 minutes per side or until just cooked through.

You could make meatballs using this mixture, either with the cheese or without. Then tuck them into your regular spaghetti and sauce.

BAKED ZITI

Baked pasta is always a crowd pleaser and this recipe is so simple, you'll be happy to please the crowd.

1 box rigatoni, penne, or ziti (make my day, make it whole wheat)

1 recipe I Don't Feel the Least Bit Guilty: All-Purpose (Perfectly Smooth) Tomato Carrot Sauce (page 29)

4 cauliflower florets, finely grated

4 ounces shredded mozzarella cheese

1/4 cup grated Parmesan cheese

Preheat the oven to 350°F. Spray or oil a 9 × 13 inch baking dish.

Cook pasta till al dente, according to the directions on the package, and drain.

Put the cooked pasta in the baking dish and drizzle sauce evenly over it. Sprinkle on cauliflower crumbles, then the mozzarella and Parmesan. Bake for 20–30 minutes or until golden and bubbly.

There are hundreds of different shapes of pasta. Plan a field trip to an Italian market in your town and let the kids pick out a few varieties.

RAINBOW CHICKEN SALAD

This is the most beautiful dish in the book. You can use a food processor fitted with the shredding blade for extra fine cabbage. Why not prep the cabbage on the weekend, put it in a bag, and keep it in the crisper drawer to make dinner a bit quicker on a school night? You can make this as a straight slaw, if that would go over better, by doubling the cabbage.

MAKES 4–6 SERVINGS

3 tablespoons rice vinegar or lime juice

2 teaspoons honey

3–4 tablespoons olive oil

$^1/_4$ head napa cabbage, finely shredded

$^1/_4$ head purple cabbage, finely shredded

2 medium carrots, julienned or grated

1 ounce Monterey Jack or Cheddar cheese, grated

1 bag of ready salad

$^1/_2$ mango, cut into $^1/_2$-inch pieces

$^1/_2$ bunch scallions, finely chopped, optional

Breast meat from rotisserie chicken, shredded (use drumsticks for lunch)

1 red bell pepper, julienned

In a small bowl, combine the vinegar, honey, and oil and stir together.

Toss remaining ingredients in a large bowl. Add dressing and toss again, adding a bit more oil or vinegar if needed. Serve immediately

Cabbage is cruciferous and full of vitamin C. Eat it often.

WHITE BEAN CHICKEN CHILI

You can never have too many do-ahead recipes or venues for beans, if you ask me! If onions are a problem, you can cook them first, then proceed as written and puree them into oblivion with the parsnips. The chilies aren't spicy, they just add a classic "green chili" flavor. Look for them near the taco kits.

MAKES 4 SERVINGS

2 medium parsnips, peeled and thinly sliced

1 cup chicken broth, divided

1 medium onion, chopped

1 pound boneless chicken breasts, cut into 1-inch pieces

3 cloves garlic, finely chopped

2 teaspoons ground cumin

One 4-ounce can diced green chilies

One 13-ounce can small white beans, such as Great Northern

1 teaspoon chili powder, optional

$1/2$ bunch scallions, chopped, optional

Chopped cilantro for garnish, optional

In a large saucepan over medium-high heat, combine the parsnips and half the chicken broth and bring to a boil. Reduce heat to a simmer and let cook about 10 minutes or until parsnips are tender. Transfer parsnips and broth to the blender, let cool slightly, and then puree until smooth.

In the same saucepan over medium heat, add just enough oil to coat the pan. Add the onions and cook about 3 minutes, making sure the onions don't color too much. Add the chicken and garlic and let cook 1 minute while stirring. Add the cumin, remaining broth, chilies, parsnip mixture, beans, and chili powder if using, and then stir. Bring to a boil.

Reduce heat and let simmer for 5 minutes. Taste and adjust seasoning. When yummy, spoon into bowls and top with scallions and cilantro, if green things are allowed in the food. Otherwise serve them at the table for the more cultivated palates.

Cilantro is a good source of vitamins A and C. If only all garnishes were!

GRILLED FISH WITH CREAMY CUCUMBER CAULIFLOWER SAUCE

This cool, refreshing dish is perfect for a summer dinner out back. For the more adventurous set, you can dust the fish with a little coriander, which works very well with the sauce.

MAKES 4 SERVINGS

Half a 10-ounce box frozen cauliflower, defrosted

$^3/_4$ cup reduced-fat sour cream or yogurt

1 teaspoon dried mint or 5–10 fresh leaves

1 chopped scallion, optional

$^1/_2$ medium cucumber, peeled, seeded, and chopped

Four 4–6 ounce fillets mild white fish (tilapia, cod, striped bass)

Steam the cauliflower in a saucepan with $^1/_2$ cup water until tender, about 8–10 minutes. Remove from the pan and let cool completely. Squeeze out any excess water.

In a mini food processor, combine the cauliflower and the sour cream or yogurt, and puree until smooth. Add the mint and scallions if using and pulse a few times. Remove sauce to a small bowl, season with salt, and stir in cucumber. Reserve refrigerated. Sauce can be made up to one day ahead.

Start up the grill or preheat a stovetop grill pan on medium-high. Lightly oil the fish. Be sure the pan or rack is hot—this will prevent sticking. Place the fish on the rack or in the pan and cook about 3–5 minutes or until you can see it turning opaque about halfway up. Turn the fish over and cook until just cooked through, about 3 minutes. Fish will continue to cook a bit after being removed. Top fish with sauce and cool off.

PICNIC PASTA SALAD

You may add any vegetables you like to this. Peppers, broccoli florets, and chopped fresh spinach would all be nice. These added vegetables will also keep the kids from noticing the vegetables going into them. The shrimp are already cooked so the pasta water will simply defrost them.

MAKES 4 SERVINGS

1 pound box of bowtie pasta

8 ounces frozen precooked shrimp

One 4-ounce jar marinated artichoke hearts

1–2 tablespoons olive oil

1 tablespoon rice vinegar

1–3 tablespoons chicken or vegetable broth

1 bunch asparagus, cut into 1-inch pieces

10–12 leaves fresh basil, chopped (combined immediately with tomatoes)

$1/2$ pint grape tomatoes, halved

3–4 tablespoons Parmesan cheese, grated

Get your pasta going according to the directions on the package. Place the shrimp in the pasta colander in the sink.

Put the artichokes, olive oil, and vinegar in the blender and puree until smooth. Add a little broth and puree again to achieve desired consistency to cover the pasta. Taste and season with salt, if desired.

When the pasta is 2 minutes from being done, drop the asparagus into the pasta water. Drain the pasta and asparagus over the shrimp. Place the pasta, shrimp, and asparagus in a large bowl, toss with remaining ingredients, and refrigerate. Reserve any extra dressing to toss with pasta just before serving if needed.

PORK CHOPS WITH PARSNIP GRAVY

You could probably make kohlrabi, cauliflower, or carrot gravy, but I picked parsnips.

2 medium parsnips, peeled and thinly sliced

1 cup chicken broth

4 center-cut pork chops, excess fat trimmed

1–2 tablespoons soy sauce

2 cloves garlic, finely chopped

1 tablespoon butter

In a saucepan over medium-high heat, cook the parsnips with ¹/₂ the chicken broth until parsnips are tender, about 10 minutes.

Place parsnips and broth in the blender and puree until smooth. Reserve.

Preheat a large, heavy skillet (preferably *not* nonstick) over medium-high heat. Splash the pork chops with the soy sauce. Add just enough oil to the pan to coat the bottom, then add the chops and give the pan a shake to ensure they aren't sticking. Let the chops brown well, about 3 minutes, then turn. When the chops have gotten a bit of color on the bottom, after about 2 minutes, remove them from the pan. Add the garlic and cook 30 seconds, then add the remaining chicken broth and stir up all the lovely brown bits on the bottom of the pan. Reduce the heat to low and add the parsnip puree. Stir in the butter and taste. If you would like the gravy to be browner, add a little splash of soy sauce; otherwise, just add salt if needed. When gravy is yummy, return chops to the pan to finish cooking, about 1 minute. Serve dinner and enjoy, without looking smug.

ARROZ VERDE CON POLLO

This is green, but you most certainly can't find any vegetables in here! This dish has a nice traditional flavor. Not everybody loves cilantro, but in this dish it's cooked and the flavor becomes quite mild.

MAKES 4 SERVINGS

1 medium onion, quartered

2 cloves garlic

One 4-ounce can diced green chilies

1 green bell pepper, stem, seeds, and ribs removed, chopped

$^1/_2$ bunch cilantro

Juice of 1 lime

$^1/_4$ cup water

4 chicken thighs

1 cup long grain rice

1$^1/_2$ cups chicken broth

In the blender, combine the onion, garlic, green chilies, green pepper, cilantro, lime juice, and water. Puree until smooth and reserve.

Heat a soup pot or large saucepan over medium-high heat, add just enough oil to coat the bottom of the pan, then brown the chicken on all sides. Remove from the pan and reserve. Add the rice and cook about 2 minutes, stirring occasionally. Add the mixture from the blender, season with salt, and cook about 1 minute. Return the chicken to the pot and add the chicken broth. Bring to a boil, then reduce the heat to a simmer and cover for 20 minutes, adding more water if needed. Remove from the heat and let stand, covered, for 10 minutes. *Olé!*

CHAMPIONSHIP CHILI

This chili has an authentic flavor and works well with the sweet potato. It's sure to become a family favorite. Since chili always tastes better the second time around, make a double recipe and freeze half.

MAKES 6 SERVINGS

1 ½ cups chicken broth

1 sweet potato, peeled and cut into 1-inch cubes

2 medium onions, finely chopped

6 cloves garlic, finely chopped

1 pound lean ground beef or turkey

1 tablespoon ground cumin

1 teaspoon chipotle puree or chili powder, optional

One 13-ounce can crushed tomatoes (pureed if necessary)

Two 4-ounce cans diced green chilies

One 13-ounce can pinto or kidney beans, drained

½ bunch scallions, chopped, optional

1 cup reduced-fat sour cream, optional

Grated Cheddar cheese, optional

Chopped fresh cilantro, optional

In a small saucepan over medium-high heat, bring the broth and sweet potatoes to a boil. Reduce to a simmer and let cook until sweet potatoes are tender, about 10 minutes. Set aside to cool (while you chop other ingredients), then puree in the blender until smooth.

Heat a Dutch oven over medium-high heat, adding just enough oil to coat the bottom of the pan. Add the onions and cook for about 3 minutes. Add garlic and cook another minute. Add the ground meat and season with salt and pepper. Brown the meat well and drain any excess fat. Add sweet potato mixture, cumin, chipotle or chili powder if using, tomatoes, green chilies, beans, and a little more salt, then stir well. Bring to a boil, then let simmer 45 minutes, tasting and adjusting the seasonings. Serve with desired toppings.

CHICKEN WITH CREAMY CAULIFLOWER SAUCE

There's nothing families like better than creamy white things on their plates. This sauce can be made ahead and frozen for quick use on a night when you gave it all at the office. Serve this with an obvious green vegetable to flaunt and make your plate more attractive.

MAKES 4 SERVINGS

Rice or noodles to serve under or alongside the chicken (but not touching it!)

One 10-ounce box frozen cauliflower, defrosted, or ½ head fresh, cut into florets

3 tablespoons reduced-fat sour cream or plain yogurt

¼ cup chicken broth

4 boneless chicken breasts, cut into 1-inch cubes

2 cloves garlic, finely chopped

Get your rice or noodles going according to the directions on the package.

Steam the cauliflower in a saucepan with a little water until tender, about 8 minutes. Place in the blender with the sour cream or yogurt and the broth, and puree until smooth. Season with salt and reserve. Sauce can be refrigerated for up to 3 days or may be frozen.

Heat a skillet over medium-high heat, adding just enough oil to coat the bottom of the pan. Add the chicken, season with salt, and brown slightly. Add garlic and cook another 30 seconds. Pour cauliflower mixture over the chicken and stir well. Bring to a boil, then reduce heat to just a simmer and cook 5 minutes or until chicken is cooked through. Taste and adjust seasoning. Serve with noodles or rice.

Make chicken broth ice cubes and keep them in an airtight zipper bag in the freezer to use when recipes call for small quantities.

SHEPHERD'S PIE

You could make this with No Trick, Just Treat Halloween Mashed Potatoes (page 70) for a simple do-ahead meal on a busy night, like Halloween.

2 medium carrots, peeled and thinly sliced

$^1/_2$ cup chicken broth

1 medium onion, chopped

1 pound lean ground beef or turkey

$^1/_4$ cup ketchup

1 tablespoon Worcestershire sauce

1 recipe Covert Cauliflower Mashed Potatoes (page 57)

2 parsnips, peeled and sliced

1 cup fresh green beans or frozen, defrosted

$^1/_4$ cup Parmesan cheese

Preheat the oven to 375°F. Butter or spray a 9 × 9 inch baking dish.

Place carrots in the blender with the chicken broth and puree until only tiny pieces of carrot remain. If your family is particularly aware, steam the carrots until tender first, so that they completely disappear. You may put the onion in at the same time, if desired.

Heat a large skillet over medium-high heat, adding just enough oil to coat the bottom of the pan, then sauté the onions until they start to brown. Add the ground beef, season with salt, and brown well. Drain any excess fat from the pan and add the carrot mixture, ketchup, and Worcestershire sauce, then stir well. Reduce heat and cook another 10 minutes, then taste and adjust seasoning. When yummy, remove from heat.

Layer about $^1/_3$ of the mashed potatoes on the bottom of the baking dish. Top with ground meat mixture and strew with parsnips and green beans. Spread remaining mashed potatoes over the top. Sprinkle with Parmesan and place in the oven for 30–40 minutes or until the top is golden brown.

SO, JUST EAT THE CHICKEN SALAD LETTUCE WRAPS

This is a fun way to eat an old favorite. There is actually nutrition in leaf lettuce, unlike ol' iceberg. Hard to believe you can't detect the kohlrabi, but you can't! Just don't let them see you throw back your head and laugh maniacally, though.

MAKES 4–6 SERVINGS

2 cooked boneless skinless chicken breasts (grilled, sautéed, or purchased)

2 stalks celery, finely chopped

1 Granny Smith apple, cut into $^1/_4$-inch cubes

1 kohlrabi, peeled, tops and bottoms removed, and cut into $^1/_4$-inch cubes

$^1/_2$ cup slivered almonds or walnuts

3–4 tablespoons I Call It Dreamy: Creamy Sandwich Spread (page 18)
  or mayonnaise

4 scallions, finely chopped, optional but really yummy

6–8 leaves of leaf lettuce

Cut the chicken into $^1/_2$-inch pieces. Combine everything except the lettuce in a medium bowl and toss. Season with salt, and taste.

Place a spoonful of the chicken salad along the center of a leaf of lettuce and roll like a burrito. If sending to school for lunch, leave the lettuce and chicken salad separate and let them roll wraps at lunchtime to ensure the lettuce stays crisp.

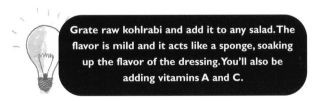

Grate raw kohlrabi and add it to any salad. The flavor is mild and it acts like a sponge, soaking up the flavor of the dressing. You'll also be adding vitamins A and C.

LINGUINI WITH ARUGULA "PESTO"

Arugula is cruciferous—there's that word again! These days you hear much about this family of vegetables because of all the health benefits associated with them. Arugula is green and, as such, very difficult to disguise, but if your family likes traditional basil pesto you can call it pesto with a straight face. This dish does have a slightly sophisticated flavor, but as you know, you just never know what they will or won't go for.

MAKES 4 SERVINGS

I pound box linguini

I head arugula, large stems trimmed

$^1/_2$ bunch basil leaves

2 tablespoons olive oil

2–3 tablespoons chicken or vegetable broth

I clove garlic, chopped

I tablespoon butter, optional

3 tablespoons pine nuts, optional

Grated Parmesan cheese, as desired

Get the linguini going according to the directions on the package.

If you'd like bright green pesto, put a saucepan on medium-high heat and bring salted water to a boil. Dunk the arugula and basil in the water for 10 seconds, then remove to an ice-water bath to stop the cooking and preserve the color. Drain and pat dry. You may skip this step for ease and will find your pesto less green but just as yummy.

In a food processor or blender, puree the arugula, basil, olive oil, chicken broth, and garlic until smooth. Season with salt, and pulse a few more times to combine. Taste and adjust seasoning.

When linguini is done, drain and return to the pot. Add pesto and toss to coat. Add the butter and pine nuts if using and toss again. Transfer to plates and top with Parmesan.

SLOPPY JOES WITH CARROTS

Relive those great moments of childhood while your children devour these. This sauce is used in a few other recipes, so you'll want to make a double batch and freeze half.

MAKES 6 SERVINGS

2 medium carrots, peeled and thinly sliced

One 15-ounce can crushed tomatoes

1 medium onion, chopped

2 cloves garlic, chopped

1 pound lean ground beef or turkey

1 tablespoon Worcestershire sauce

3 tablespoons ketchup

1 tablespoon brown sugar

6 buns, whole grain if possible, toasted

In a large skillet over medium heat cook the carrots and the tomatoes about 10 minutes or until the carrots are tender. Let cool slightly and then puree in the blender until smooth (chunks of carrot like to hide in the bottom, so keep an eye out). If concerned about strong onion flavor or if the kids pick the onions out of their food, you could cook the onions with the carrots and tomatoes and proceed as above.

In the same pan over medium-high heat, add just enough oil to coat the bottom of the pan, then add the onion and cook until golden. Add the garlic and cook another minute. Add the ground beef or turkey, season with salt, and brown well. Drain any excess fat from the pan and add tomato mixture, Worcestershire sauce, ketchup, and brown sugar, then stir well. Let simmer 10 minutes, then taste and adjust seasoning. Serve over toasted buns.

SLOPPY POTATO SKINS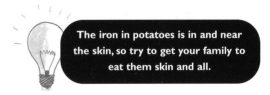

This recipe is at least as tasty as the chain-restaurant fare, but won't shorten your life. It's a no-fuss dinner if you've got some Sloppy Joe mixture in the freezer ready to go.

MAKES 4 SERVINGS

2 medium Idaho potatoes, well scrubbed

1 recipe Sloppy Joe sauce (page 106)

1 ounce Cheddar or mozzarella cheese, grated

Preheat the oven to 400°F.

Pierce the potatoes with a fork and place in the oven. Bake for about 45 minutes or until tender at the center (check with a paring knife). Remove from the oven and let cool slightly.

Heat the Sloppy Joe sauce in a saucepan over medium heat. Slice potatoes in half lengthwise and place on plates. Top with Sloppy Joe sauce and cheese. Enjoy the sound of a peaceful, happy dinner table.

> The iron in potatoes is in and near the skin, so try to get your family to eat them skin and all.

KOHLRABI SPAGHETTI AND SLOPPY JOE SAUCE

Kohlrabi is cruciferous and therefore especially high on my "must eat" list. You have to be knee-deep in writing a cookbook about vegetables to come up with this recipe, but I'll tell you, it's delicious. It requires investing in a spiral slicer. I must say, though, that once you start playing with it you'll just keep finding things you want to spiral slice, and the kids will love it. The slightly sweet Sloppy Joe sauce works a bit better with the kohlrabi than spaghetti sauce, but either would be fine.

MAKES 4 SERVINGS

I recipe Sloppy Joe sauce (page 106)
4 kohlrabi, peeled, tops and bottoms removed, and spiral sliced

Heat the Sloppy Joe sauce in a saucepan over medium heat.

In a large skillet over medium heat, bring about 3 tablespoons of water and the kohlrabi to a simmer, letting the kohlrabi cook about 3 minutes and adding more water if needed. Drain any remaining water from the kohlrabi and place on plates. Top with Sloppy Joe mixture. Watch the look of amazement when they discover two-foot-long "noodles" under the sauce.

Cruciferous vegetables seem to help our bodies fight cancer thanks to the isothiocyanates, sulforaphane, and indole-3-carbinol they contain. Just remember to eat them and forget the big words.

SAUTÉED TILAPIA WITH SALSA

Most children will eat mild fish like tilapia. It is found in most grocery stores these days, and because it cooks so quickly, it makes a great choice on busy nights. Any mild white fish would be fine, however. If you need to entice them with a bit more flavor, substitute 1 tablespoon of butter for the oil when cooking.

MAKES 4 SERVINGS

Four 4–6 ounce tilapia fillets
1 tablespoon cornmeal or all-purpose flour, optional
$1/2$–1 cup favorite salsa

Heat a large sauté pan over medium-high heat. Season the fish with salt. If you are concerned about the fish sticking, dust the fillets with cornmeal (corn is a vegetable!) or flour. Add just enough oil to coat the bottom of the pan, then add the fish. Give the pan a shake to ensure that the fish isn't sticking. Cook 2–3 minutes or until the fish has turned opaque halfway up. Turn the fillets over and let cook on the other side until just cooked through, about another 2–3 minutes (the fish will continue to cook after it comes out of the pan, so avoid overcooking it in the pan).

Transfer fish to plates and top with salsa. Serve alongside a vegetable that you ask them to try.

HEY, PARDNER, WANT A SEEMINGLY "ONIONLESS" WESTERN OMELET?)

Onions are good for you, but kids pick out millions of onion nubbins every year and put them aside. This is a real tragedy because onions seem to ward off a host of health troubles and help lower cholesterol. It's never too soon to think about that. Let the kids pick out the peppers.

MAKES 4 SERVINGS

1 medium onion, chopped

1 tablespoon butter, or as needed

8 large eggs

$\frac{1}{2}$ red bell pepper, finely chopped

$\frac{1}{2}$ green bell pepper, finely chopped

2 ounces Cheddar, mozzarella, or Monterey Jack cheese, grated

Salsa or ketchup, optional

In an 8-inch nonstick skillet or omelet pan over medium heat, cook the onions in a dot of butter until they're just starting to turn golden. Remove to the blender, add the eggs, and season with salt. Puree until the onions have disappeared.

Return the pan to the heat. Add another dot of butter, if needed, and about $\frac{1}{4}$ of the peppers. Cook for 1 minute, then add $\frac{1}{4}$ of the eggs. Using a heat-resistant rubber spatula, hold the handle of the pan with one hand and stir the eggs with the spatula in the other hand. When the eggs start to set, after about a minute, stop stirring and top with $\frac{1}{4}$ of the cheese, and then partially cover the pan with a lid. Cook until eggs are set, about 2 minutes, then scrape along the edges with the rubber spatula to make sure the omelet isn't sticking. Roll out onto a plate so that the omelet folds into thirds. Top with salsa or ketchup if desired. Repeat three times with remaining ingredients. You can keep the omelets warm on a sheet pan for up to 20 minutes in a 300°F oven, then transfer them to plates for serving.

Because ketchup contains cooked tomatoes, it is a good source of lycopene, Squirt away!

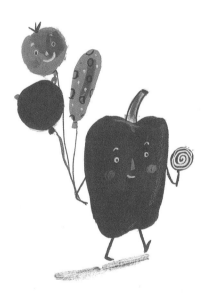

JERUSALEM ARTICHOKE PASTA WITH NO-SEE-UM SPAGHETTI SAUCE

You probably didn't know there was Jerusalem artichoke pasta. It is found in most health food stores and many traditional grocery stores these days. De Boles pasta is made with Jerusalem artichokes but not labeled as such on the front. It isn't a huge improvement over regular pasta, but as we say, every little bit helps. This sauce is silky smooth with no icky onion bits.

MAKES 4 SERVINGS

1 box Jerusalem artichoke pasta (any shape)
1 jar spaghetti sauce

Get the pasta going according to the directions on the package.

Put the spaghetti sauce in the blender and puree until smooth, then place in a saucepan over medium heat. When pasta is cooked and drained, pour the heated sauce on top.

To make meat sauce, heat 1 pound of ground beef or turkey in a large skillet over medium-high heat. Brown the meat well, then add pureed sauce and stir to combine. Serve over cooked, drained pasta.

Rotate your toxins! This is one of my guiding tenets of eating. If you never eat too much of any one food, it can't kill you, so eating a variety of foods is important. Which is why I'm asking you to eat Jerusalem artichoke pasta.

MACARONI AND CHEESE WITH MOONS AND STARS

How many generations of children would have starved to death if it weren't for mac and cheese? How lovely if we got a couple of vegetables into them while preventing starvation. Thankfully there are brands of mac and cheese that have only recognizable ingredients. Hopefully your family enjoys them. This recipe calls for moons and stars, but you may, of course, use any shape you like—just keep them tiny.

MAKES 4 SERVINGS

$1/2$ red bell pepper, top and bottom trimmed, seeds removed
$1/2$ orange bell pepper, top and bottom trimmed, seeds removed
1 box of the family favorite mac and cheese

Quarter the peppers and lay them skin side down on a cutting board. Using $1/2$-inch moon and star cookie cutters, cut out 6–12 of each shape.

Prepare the mac and cheese according to the directions on the box. Either stir in the moons and stars or artistically arrange them on top of the mac and cheese. If cooked peppers are preferred, drop into the cooking macaroni for the last 2 minutes of cooking time.

Make a few extra moons and stars, or keep any you have left over, to use as garnish on another meal—now that they know they like them.

PITA-DILLAS WITH CARROT TOMATO SAUCE

The hope is that on a day when you have some energy you will have made a batch of Tomato Carrot Sauce to be used on another day when you come home burned out from the office. A pita-dilla is a cross between a quesadilla and a tostada, made with pitas instead of tortillas, but you can call it anything you like.

4 whole-wheat pitas

1–2 cups I Don't Feel the Least Bit Guilty: All-Purpose (Perfectly Smooth) Tomato Carrot Sauce (page 29)

4 ounces mozzarella cheese, grated

8 ounces cooked chicken or canned tuna, optional

Frozen spinach, defrosted and squeezed, optional (I can dream, can't I?)

Preheat the broiler or the toaster oven.

Place each pita on a baking sheet and top with a little sauce. Divide cheese between pitas and finish off with any other toppings your family likes. Add spinach if using (sigh). Add another splash of sauce, depending on everyone's preference.

Place in the toaster oven or under the broiler for about 1 minute or until cheese has melted and is starting to turn golden. Remove from oven and let cool 1 minute before cutting into quarters, or serve whole.

PIZZA WITH CAULIFLOWER CRUMBLES

No steaming, no pureeing—just hiding it under the cheese!

As always, start bumping up the amount of cauliflower after you get this into them a few times. They can help assemble these when young enough to be fooled by referring to the "first cheese" and "second cheese," if you like. As mentioned previously, helping with preparation creates a desire for consumption.

4 mini ready pizza crusts

$^1/_2$–1 cup pizza sauce

4 cauliflower florets, grated (use the smallest holes on the grater)

4 ounces mozzarella cheese, grated

2 tablespoons grated Parmesan cheese

Favorite toppings as desired

Preheat the broiler, or set the toaster oven to the highest possible temperature.

Place the crusts on a baking sheet and top with a little sauce. Divide cauliflower between pizzas and finish off with cheeses and any other toppings your family likes. Add another splash of sauce, depending on everyone's preference.

Place in the toaster oven or under the broiler for about 1 minute or until the cheese has melted and is starting to turn golden. Remove from oven and let cool briefly before cutting into quarters, or serve whole.

I WON'T *DESSERT*
THE MISSION, EVEN
AFTER DINNER

DESSERTS

PUMPKIN WALNUT LOAF

Not only a tasty dessert, this pumpkin walnut loaf is a great lunch-box treat. Although I s'pose they might trade it for something more attractive to them. As long as *some* child is eating more healthfully, I'll be happy.

2 cups brown sugar, firmly packed

One 12-ounce can pumpkin puree

1/2 cup canola or grape seed oil

2 large eggs, lightly beaten

2 teaspoons baking soda

1 teaspoon ground cinnamon

1 teaspoon ground ginger

A few grates of nutmeg

1/2 teaspoon salt

1 cup chopped walnuts

2 1/2 cups all-purpose flour

Preheat oven to 350°F. Butter and flour a loaf pan.

In a large bowl, add everything but the flour and mix well. Add the flour and stir until just combined and no large lumps of flour remain.

Pour into buttered pan and bake about 40 minutes or until a toothpick inserted in the middle of the loaf comes out clean. Let cool in the pan for 10 minutes, then remove to a rack to finish cooling.

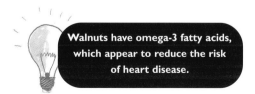

Walnuts have omega-3 fatty acids, which appear to reduce the risk of heart disease.

SWEET POTATO PIE WITH GINGER AND ORANGE

The natural sweetness of the sweet potatoes is very kid friendly and the orange gives this pie a nice brightness. Add a cup of chopped nuts if you like.

2 large sweet potatoes (about 1 1/2 pounds)

3/4 cup milk

2 large eggs

1/2 cup brown sugar

1 tablespoon butter, softened

1 teaspoon vanilla

Juice and zest of 1 orange

1 teaspoon ground ginger

1 teaspoon salt

One 9-inch pie shell

Preheat the oven to 375°F.

Scrub the potatoes and pierce with a fork. Bake for 45 minutes to 1 hour or until tender when poked with a paring knife. Let cool, then peel and mash. Reset the oven to 425°F.

In a large mixing bowl, combine remaining ingredients (except the crust!) and stir together until smooth. Pour into pie shell and bake for 15 minutes. Without opening the oven door, lower the temperature to 350°F and continue baking for another 40–45 minutes, or until the center is set (a paring knife inserted in the center should come out clean). Remove from oven and let cool.

Pure vanilla extract actually improves with age, so if you're worrying about how old that bottle is, don't!

CARROT CAKE

This one doesn't need any explaining, but I will tell you it can be frozen so that you don't feel like you have to eat the whole thing.

4 large eggs, lightly beaten

2 cups brown sugar

Pinch salt

³/₄ cup canola or grape seed oil

¹/₂ cup buttermilk

3¹/₂ cups all-purpose flour

1¹/₂ teaspoons baking powder

¹/₂ teaspoon baking soda

1 teaspoon ground cinnamon

A few grates fresh nutmeg

¹/₂ teaspoon ground ginger

5 cups grated carrots (about 10–12 medium)

1 cup chopped walnuts

1 recipe I Did Consider Putting Parsnips in Here, But...Cream Cheese Frosting (page 120)

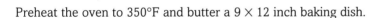

Preheat the oven to 350°F and butter a 9 × 12 inch baking dish.

In a mixing bowl, combine the eggs, brown sugar, salt, oil, and buttermilk. Beat with a mixer for about 30 seconds or by hand for 3 minutes.

In another medium bowl, combine the flour, baking powder, baking soda, and the spices, then stir to combine.

With the mixer running or while stirring, add the dry ingredients to the butter and egg mixture until just combined. Fold in the carrots and nuts and pour into the baking dish, smoothing the top.

Bake for 30–40 minutes or until springy in the center. Let cool completely. Gently spread frosting over the top of the cake.

CREAM CHEESE FROSTING

¹/₂ stick butter, softened

8 ounces cream cheese, softened

¹/₂–³/₄ cup sugar

1 teaspoon vanilla

In a mixing bowl, combine the butter and cream cheese with a mixer or by hand until smooth. Add the sugar to taste and vanilla and continue mixing until very smooth. Don't eat it all before the cake is done!

ZUCCHINI MUFFINS

If you use the cute paper liners and splurge on the I Did Consider Putting Parsnips in Here, But...Cream Cheese Frosting (page 120), they really will be cupcakes.

MAKES 12 "CUPCAKES"

I large egg

$^{1}/_{2}$ cup plain yogurt

$^{1}/_{3}$ cup oil

I cup grated zucchini (about I medium)

I cup all-purpose flour

I cup quick-cooking oats

$^{3}/_{4}$ cup brown sugar

I tablespoon baking powder

Pinch salt

A few grates nutmeg

I cup chopped walnuts

Preheat the oven to 375°F. Line or spray twelve muffin cups.

In a medium mixing bowl, stir together the egg, yogurt, oil, and zucchini.

In another medium bowl, mix together the flour, oats, sugar, baking powder, salt, and nutmeg. Stir dry ingredients into wet mixture until just combined—don't overmix. Fold in the nuts and divide mixture between muffin cups.

Bake 15–20 minutes or until springy and a toothpick inserted comes out clean. Muffins will keep several days in an airtight container.

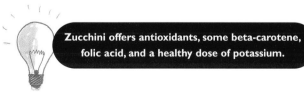

Zucchini offers antioxidants, some beta-carotene, folic acid, and a healthy dose of potassium.

PUMPKIN SMOOTHIE

Feel free to try other fruits, but blueberries or raspberries will help the color, which can come out all wrong with certain fruit combinations.

MAKES 2 SERVINGS

2 scoops vanilla ice cream
¹/₂ cup pumpkin puree
1 cup frozen blueberries
Squirt of honey, if needed
¹/₄ cup buttermilk
Milk, as needed (about ¹/₂ cup)

In a blender combine everything except the milk and pulse several times. Add a little milk and puree until smooth, adding more milk as needed to achieve desired consistency.

PUMPKIN BREAD PUDDING

You can use leftover dinner rolls to make this treat. Even if your kids are not fans of pumpkin pie, which can be overly spiced, the whole family will enjoy this pumpkin bread pudding. It can be lovingly served with vanilla ice cream, chocolate sauce, or applesauce.

MAKES 6–8 SERVINGS

$1/2$ pound whole-wheat rolls (about 4–6), or white if you must

$1/2$ cup pumpkin puree

2 large eggs

$1/4$ cup buttermilk

$1/2$ cup milk

A few grates of fresh nutmeg

$1/2$ teaspoon cinnamon

$1/2$ teaspoon vanilla

$1/2$ cup brown sugar, plus some for sprinkling on top

Preheat the oven to 350°F. Spray or butter a 9 × 9 inch baking dish.

In a large mixing bowl, rip the rolls into 1-inch pieces.

In a medium mixing bowl, whisk together the remaining ingredients (except the brown sugar for sprinkling on top) and a tiny pinch of salt. Pour over the bread and fold together until all the bread is coated. Spread the mixture evenly in the baking dish, sprinkle a little more brown sugar on top, and bake for 35–40 minutes or until golden brown and slightly springy. Serve warm!

PUMPKIN BUTTERSCOTCH PUDDING

If you're concerned about detection, you could make this pudding with half the pumpkin to start with, then bump it up each time you make it. I can never decide if I like this recipe better warm or chilled. It is quick enough to make after dinner if you don't have time before—and who does?

MAKES 6 SERVINGS

4 large egg yolks

$^3/_4$ cup packed brown sugar

Scant $^1/_4$ cup cornstarch

2$^1/_2$ cups milk, divided

$^1/_2$ cup pumpkin puree

2 tablespoons cold butter

2 tablespoons vanilla

Whipped cream for garnish, optional

In a medium mixing bowl, whisk together yolks, brown sugar, cornstarch, $^1/_2$ cup milk, and the pumpkin until well mixed and smooth.

Put the remaining milk in a medium saucepan and bring to just under a boil. Remove from the heat and whisk about $^1/_2$ cup of the hot milk into the egg mixture. Whisk the entire warmed egg mixture into the saucepan with the hot milk and return to a medium flame. Stirring constantly, bring mixture to a boil and let cook for 2 minutes. Remove from heat and stir in butter and vanilla. Pour into serving dishes, and serve warm or chilled. It would be delicious slathered warm over Quit Your Loafin' and Eat This Pumpkin Walnut Loaf (page 117) for a sweet doubleheader.

JICAMA "FRIES" AND RASPBERRY "KETCHUP"

Jicama is naturally sweet and has wonderful crunch as well as a nice dose of vitamin C and fiber. Use the remaining jicama in salads. You can give fresh strawberries the same treatment, but omit the lemon juice.

Half a 10-ounce bag frozen raspberries, defrosted
Squeeze of lemon juice
1–3 tablespoons sugar
¼ jicama, peeled and cut into "fry" shapes

To make the "ketchup," place the raspberries in the blender with the lemon juice and puree until smooth. Add 1–2 tablespoons of sugar and pulse several times to incorporate. Taste and decide if it needs more sugar, adding more if desired. Strain the seeds out using a mesh sieve, if desired. This freezes well and will keep in the fridge for one week.

Put the fries on a plate with a little bowl of "ketchup" in the middle. Start dipping!

Jicama would seem to be a worthless watery vegetable, but it actually has some iron, vitamin E, folate, manganese, and thiamine as well. Serve "fries" with dinner for a nice little something crunchy.

ABOUT THE AUTHOR

Chris Fisk is a cooking teacher, consulting chef, and caterer in New York City. She is Cooking Class Coordinator for Williams-Sonoma New York City, and founded Culinary Explorers, a cooking school in Manhattan. She has developed recipes for major food companies (she probably wrote one of the recipes in your cupboard) and has written for *Parenting* magazine.

With a Blue Ribbon diploma from The Institute of Culinary Education, formerly Peter Kump's New York Cooking School, Chris has worked in restaurants and hotels in New York and around the country. Nothing makes her happier than hearing that one of her recipes has made it into someone's weekly lineup.

Prior to attending cooking school, Chris graduated from Ringling Bros. And Barnum & Bailey Clown College, so think twice about taking a pie class from her! Feel free to contact her: ClownChef@yahoo.com.

INDEX